36 Bottles of Wine

PAUL ZITARELLI

36
BOTTLES
OF
WINE

**Less Is More with 3 Recommended Wines
per Month Plus Seasonal Recipe Pairings**

SASQUATCH BOOKS
SEATTLE

MAY

Austrian Grüner Veltliner 63
Oregon Pinot Noir 64
Tokaji Aszú 5 Puttonyos 69

May Meal:
Shioyaki Salmon with Pea Salad 71

JUNE

Savoie Blanc 77
Côte de Brouilly 78
Cava 83

June Meal:
Saffron-Butter Spot Prawns with
a Simple Salad with Honey-Fish
Sauce Dressing and Strawberries 85

JULY

Rías Baixas Albariño 93
California Zinfandel 94
Côtes de Provence Rosé 97

July Meal:
Red-Blooded American
Cheeseburger with Grilled
Corn 100

AUGUST

Muscadet 109
Chinon Rouge 110
Getariako Txakolina 113

August Meal:
Oysters Three Ways 114

Grignan-les-Adhémar

Certain explanations for why regions produce value wines turn up time and time again. Cheap labor, swings of fashion, fancier neighboring regions: all common. Considerably less common? Nuclear accidents.

Grignan-les-Adhémar was not always Grignan-les-Adhémar. From its inception as a wine appellation in 1973, the region was known as Coteaux du Tricastin. For decades, it hummed along as a little insider darling, mostly consumed by the French and the British.

Then, in July 2008, disaster. An accident at the Tricastin nuclear power plant. (I envision a Gallic Homer Simpson—*oh-mer seemp-sohn*—supervising operations, deep in the oblivion of a post-pâté-and-cornichons-lunch nap.) Nearly five thousand gallons of uranium solution released. In addition to the obvious contamination to the surrounding land and rivers, a less obvious contamination revealed itself over time: to the name *Tricastin*.

Winemakers were horrified to see sales begin to slip in 2008 and 2009. They tried what they could. Geiger counters in the vineyards with news crews in tow. Shrinking the label font of "Coteaux du Tricastin" to magnifying-glass levels. Nothing worked, because apparently our ape brains just cannot stop engaging the flight response from a word that *reminds* us of something dangerous. So the Tricastin winemakers settled on a more radical solution. A total reset. A name change. They petitioned the French governing body for a change to Grignan-les-Adhémar (rolls right off the tongue), and by summer 2010 (the blink of an eye by French wine bureaucracy standards), the name change was approved.

When these wines were called Coteaux du Tricastin, they were fine values. But building up a new name from scratch: that requires aggressive tactics (read: aggressive pricing), so the values have become even more compelling. Furthermore, exports to the United States have recently increased, making the wines more readily available, as producers bet on a market whose customers wouldn't know Tricastin from Pakistan.

This is the northernmost region in the Southern Rhône, so it occupies a transition zone between the full-bodied Grenache of the south (think

GRIGNAN-LES-ADHÉMAR

WHAT	Dry red blend made mostly from Grenache and Syrah
WHERE	The northern edge of the Southern Rhône Valley in southern France
WHY	A nuclear accident in 2008 forced this region to undergo a name change and decrease prices, making the wines excellent values.
PRONUNCIATION	*GREEN-yahn-layz-AH-deh-mar*
HOW MUCH	Decent examples cost $10 to $20.
PAIR WITH	Cassoulet or any simple sausage and bean stew

AMONTILLADO

WHAT	A style of dry Sherry, fortified wine made from the white grape variety Palomino
WHERE	Jerez, southern Spain
WHY	This salty, nutty acquired taste is unlike any other wine in the world, making it a marvel for both cooking and drinking.
PRONUNCIATION	*ah-mohn-tee-YAH-doh*
HOW MUCH	Decent examples cost $10 to $20.
PAIR WITH	A charcuterie and cheese plate, preferably one that includes a small pile of marcona almonds

Châteauneuf-du-Pape) and the lighter, earthier Syrahs of the Northern Rhône. The resulting blends (which can also include Mourvèdre, Cinsault, and Carignan) hit the trinity of Grenache notes (brambly berry, underbrush, mineral) while also conveying Syrah's earthy tones—subtleties that remind some of *truffes du Tricastin*, the famous black truffles of the region, which, fear not, are neither abnormally large nor glow in the dark.

Amontillado

Good bone-dry Amontillado sits at the intersection of salty and nutty (if you like peanut butter, chances are you'll come around to Amontillado). Slowly sipping a glass while nibbling on a plate of charcuterie and hard cheeses and salted nuts, that's a fine way to pass many a dark winter hour. Despite my best efforts, it seems most Americans still favor beer and hot wings for Super Bowl parties instead of Amontillado and cured meats. But I'll keep banging the drum.

This style of Sherry is beyond love-it-or-hate-it. It's more like love-it-or-hate-it-or-hate-it-at-first-but-then-find-yourself-thinking-about-it-two-weeks-later-and-wanting-to-try-it-again-and-then-dammit-I-kind-of-like-this-why-do-I-like-this-and-then-okay-I-need-Amontillado-in-the-house-at-all-times-along-with-a-steady-supply-of-marcona-almonds-and-*jamón-serrano*. It's polarizing. It's the definition of an acquired taste. And it's about as far from sweet-Sherry-as-Grandma's-bedtime-tipple as you can get.

It's also unlike any other wine in the world, in no small part because winemakers in Jerez (in southern Spain, closer to Morocco than France or Portugal) expose their wines to practices that are considered atrocities in nearly every other winemaking region: lousy grapes, underfilled barrels, funky yeasts, and oxygen exposure.

Sherry winemakers begin with the Palomino grape. Main selling point: insipid neutrality. Palomino makes exceptionally dull white wine, which in most places would be considered a negative, but in Jerez is perfect as a blank canvas for the horrors to follow. Makers of Amontillado ferment their boring Palomino to dryness, fill their barrels to only about 80 percent of capacity, then add a neutral spirit to fortify the wine to an alcohol level that encourages the formation of *flor*, the benevolent film-forming yeast of Jerez. Flor is benevolent because a) unlike many yeasts that turn up in barrels, this one *does not* make the finished wine smell like the business end of a barnyard, but instead imparts subtle notes of bread dough and flinty, salty mineral tang; and b) the yeast film protects the wine in barrel from exposure to oxygen.

Now that our Jerez winemakers have successfully coddled their flor into existence, do they nurture their delicate yeast film? No, they do not. They allow it to die, on purpose, because for Amontillado, they actually want the wine exposed to oxygen. That oxygen exposure turns the wine brown (just like an apple left on the counter) and imparts Amontillado's signature nuttiness.

What is the result of this middling grape exposed to oddball yeast and way too much air? A wine with enough richness and high alcohol (thanks to fortification) to make it a lovely choice for wintertime. A wine that tastes like a bowlful of salted nuts (cashew, pecan), overlain with layers of marzipan and light lemony citrus. You get to taste the influence of both flor (saline yeasty notes) and oxygen (nuts, salt caramel), the two benign atrocities that make Amontillado what it is.

January Meal

Sherried Clams and Roasted Cauliflower with Sherry Vinaigrette

THE SECRET INGREDIENT

From a very young age, I remember knowing on a gut level that something differentiated a crab chowder from a crab bisque. The bisque always had this subtle, nutty (and, as I later learned, alcoholic) note that made it feel a little more grown-up than plain-jane chowder. Later in life, I discovered the reason why, the secret ingredient: Sherry.

Sherry is wine in the same way that high-cacao dark chocolate is candy. An acquired taste. Clearly meant for adults. I've learned through painful experience that the best way to introduce your newbie friends to good dry Sherry is not to pour them a slug and watch them sip with the anticipation of great revelations ahead. Nine times out of ten, the revelation turns out to be: *I don't like Sherry. This doesn't taste like wine. Why are you doing this to me?* It's true: Sherry doesn't taste like most wine. It's salty. Briny. Nutty. Atypical descriptors for most wines. Like I said: an acquired taste.

There's a noble but misguided attempt by hipster mixologists to rescue dry Sherry by incorporating it into oddball cocktails. I respect the end goal, not so much the means. Ultimately, it reminds me too much of mixing liquid Tylenol into applesauce to get my daughter to take her medicine. If it tastes good in the first place, why do we need to hide it?

The best way to offer an introduction to the glories of dry Sherry is in a hot pan. Any recipe that calls for white wine will be transmuted with a Sherry substitute. I challenge you to deglaze a red-hot pan of sautéed mushrooms and thyme with an Amontillado and not be completely seduced by the nutty cloud that will envelop your kitchen.

Sherried Clams

There's a reason that Sherry works so well with all those seafood bisques. To put it simply: salt likes salt. Seafood's natural brine is enhanced by the saltiness of a good dry Sherry. That concept is not limited only to bisques. It is also fabulous in one of my favorite one-pot midweek meals: steamed clams.

To me there is something impossibly soul-fulfilling about sitting around a table with a huge bowl of steamed clams in the middle, a communal plate piled high with a rustic loaf of toasted, buttered bread. The dipping and slurping. The mess. The satisfied groans.

Makes 4 servings

2 tablespoons unsalted butter

1 medium leek, white and light-green parts only, washed, halved lengthwise, and thinly sliced

¼ cup diced dried Spanish chorizo

1 tablespoon smoked paprika

1 cup Amontillado

1 (15-ounce) can crushed tomatoes

1 (15-ounce) can chickpeas, rinsed and drained

¼ cup whipping cream

1 baguette, halved lengthwise

Salted butter, for spreading

4 pounds Manila clams

Chopped fresh parsley, for garnish

Sauté. Preheat the oven to 350 degrees F. In a large stockpot over medium-high heat, heat the butter until any foam subsides. Add the leek and chorizo and sauté until lightly browned, 5 to 6 minutes. Stir in the paprika and cook for another minute. Resist the urge to add any salt at this stage. Many of the ingredients in this recipe are naturally salty (chorizo, Sherry, clams), so it's best to wait until the end to determine if any additional salt is needed.

Deglaze. Add the Amontillado and scrape any browned bits from the bottom of the pot. Boil until the steam smells nutty, not alcoholic (1 to 2 minutes), and then add the tomatoes, chickpeas, and cream. Increase the heat to high and return to a rolling boil.

Prepare the baguette. Arrange the baguette halves, cut side down, on a rimmed baking sheet and place in the oven. Cook until warmed through, 10 to 15 minutes, then spread copiously with butter.

Steam the clams. Add the clams to the pot, immediately cover, and leave alone for a minute. After that minute is up, hold the lid tightly on and give the pot two or three big shakes, then return it to the heat for another 30 seconds. Remove the lid and check the clams. (This is a good time to check for seasoning and see if additional salt is needed.) If the vast majority have opened, it's time to transfer them to a large bowl, either carefully with a ladle, or messily (but quickly) by dumping them in. If many of the clams are still closed, return the pot to the heat and check again after another 30 seconds. Repeat until satisfied, and note that overall cooking time will vary widely by stovetop and pan, usually falling between 90 seconds and 5 minutes.

Serve. Garnish the bowl of clams with parsley and place it in the center of the table alongside one or two shell bowls and the buttered baguette. Provide each diner with a bowl and spoon. That spoon will come in handy after they've eaten all their allotted clams, dipped all their allotted bread, and find themselves with a small serving of what looks (and tastes) like clam bisque in the bottom of their bowl.

Roasted Cauliflower
with Sherry Vinaigrette

This can be served before, after, or alongside the clams. The flavors are complementary: earthy clams and earthy cauliflower, Sherry products in both, and anchovy paste here as a sneaky callback to the sea.

Makes 4 servings

½ cup extra-virgin olive oil, divided

6 anchovy fillets, finely chopped

3 cloves garlic, minced

½ teaspoon red pepper flakes

2 tablespoons Sherry vinegar

1 large head cauliflower, separated into florets (4 to 6 cups)

Kosher salt

Chopped fresh parsley, for garnish

Make the vinaigrette. Preheat the oven to 425 degrees F. In a medium skillet over medium heat, heat ¼ cup of the olive oil. Add the anchovies, garlic, and red pepper, and cook, stirring occasionally, until the garlic softens, 4 to 8 minutes. Remove the pan from the heat and whisk in the Sherry vinegar.

Roast the cauliflower. In a large bowl, toss the cauliflower florets with the remaining ¼ cup olive oil and season lightly with salt (go easy here; the anchovies will make the vinaigrette plenty salty). Spread them in a single layer on a rimmed baking sheet and bake until golden-brown and tender, 20 to 30 minutes.

Serve. Return the florets to the large bowl, add the vinaigrette, and toss lightly. Garnish with parsley and serve warm or at room temperature; the dish is delicious either way. ▶

Substitutions and Notes: Instead of dried Spanish chorizo for the clams, you can use other dried or smoked sausages (e.g., andouille, salami). Any dry Sherry is okay as a substitute for Amontillado. Dry white wine will also work, but it will change the flavor profile considerably. If you don't want to spend time and stink up your kitchen chopping anchovies, you can substitute 3 teaspoons anchovy paste for the fillets. Finally, balsamic vinegar can work as a substitute for Sherry vinegar; it will just make the vinaigrette a touch sweeter.

Pairing: Most seafood is traditionally paired with white wines, and rightly so: the tannins present in red wine can convey metallic flavors when paired with many finfish, and robust reds tend to overwhelm the delicate flavors of many shellfish. Earthy clams are an exception, offering a fascinating pairing partner to a midweight red like Grignan-les-Adhémar. If that sounds too odd, just crack a Fiano di Avellino. It will be lovely with the clams, and its earth and spice notes will be a knockout next to the funky anchovy-studded cauliflower as well.

Unpacking Common Wine Descriptors

Some parts of wine-tasting notes are easy to understand. We all get aromas and flavors. On a gut (and nose) level, it's pretty easy to comprehend the difference between fruit notes (berries, cherries, and the like) and oak notes (vanilla, coffee, smoke). Many tasting notes actually overfocus on aromas and flavors, agonizing over whether that's a huckleberry or a marionberry when it's merely one component of what makes each wine unique.

Wine is as much about texture as it is about flavor, and textural descriptors don't come as naturally. Let's unpack the three most important categories: acid, tannin, and body.

The word *structure*, when it comes to wine, refers to both acid and tannin, which, combined, form the framing of a good bottle of wine, the bones that will support the delicious fruit and allow it to age and evolve successfully. Wine grapes all contain natural acidity, and the best way to think about acid is to compare it to seasoning in foods. The miracle of salt is that, when used judiciously, it enhances and strengthens flavors without changing them. It makes foods taste more like themselves. When salt is absent, even good, well-prepared food tastes dull, and the same is true for acidity in wines. When you see a wine described as "dull" or "flat" or "flabby," you can bet that wine has a dearth of acid. The right amount of acid makes a wine taste bright in your mouth. It enlivens flavors, cuts through rich foods, and activates the salivary glands.

Tannins (which are mostly relegated to red wines) lead to that gum- and cheek-sucking feeling of astringency, similar to oversteeped black tea. Some red wines that seem unpleasantly tannic on their own (too much of a drying sensation in the mouth) can be revelatory when paired with, say, a fatty slab of rib eye. Tannic wines go so well with steaks and other fatty foods because they effectively clean lipids off your palate. The mouth-puckering sensation that you experience while drinking a tannic wine on its own harmonizes beautifully with rich foods, each sip resetting the palate and inviting another bite.

There is a lactic rule of thumb for understanding a wine's body, which describes the overall sense of weight a wine has in the mouth. A light-bodied wine has the density of skim milk; medium-bodied, 2 percent; full-bodied, whole. If you want to know what a wine with unctuous body feels like in the mouth, you're going to have to crack your carton of whipping cream and take a swig. I won't judge.

MOSEL RIESLING KABINETT

WHAT	An off-dry (semisweet) white wine made from the grape variety Riesling
WHERE	The banks of the Mosel River as it weaves its way through western Germany
WHY	This is the greatest Riesling in the world, and its kiss of sugar makes it a super-versatile complement to food.
PRONUNCIATION	*MO-sel REES-ling KA-bee-nett*
HOW MUCH	Decent examples cost $20 to $30.
PAIR WITH	Cheap Chinese American takeout: kung pao shrimp, General Tso's chicken, greasy egg rolls

Mosel Riesling Kabinett

Wine fashion moves like the tides, and savvy drinkers know the best values come on the ebb tides. The early 1900s were Riesling's flood tide, when Riesling often occupied the most expensive spots on restaurant menus and could cost more than three times a first-growth Bordeaux. More than a century later, the quality of the grape hasn't changed; fashion has.

If you're going to drink Riesling, you might as well drink the greatest Riesling in the world, which comes from the steep slopes of the Mosel River valley in Germany. This area is special because the slate content is off the charts. Some vineyards essentially have no topsoil; the "soil" is pure broken slate, and the resulting wines burst with a mix of fruit, flower, and all the minerals you'd expect of a wine coming from a vertical slate-scape. All this on a brisk, low-alcohol (usually 8 to 10 percent) frame, with a kiss of residual sugar.

That's where the term *Kabinett* comes in, which in nearly all cases connotes an off-dry (just a little sweet) wine. Riesling's great strength is its versatility, its ability to make beautiful wines ranging from bone dry to sticky sweet. The Germans use their *Prädikat* system as rules of thumb for Riesling sweetness, ranging from Kabinett to *Spätlese* to *Auslese* to *Beerenauslese* to *Trockenbeerenauslese* (they had to stop there, because *Übertrockenbeerenauslese* wouldn't fit on a label). I say "rule of thumb" and not "rule" because the system actually measures the sugar content of the *grapes* at harvest time, not of the *finished wine*.

But for the vast majority of cases, the rule of thumb works, and if you pick up most Kabinetts from the Mosel, you can expect an off-dry wine. The reason to choose a Kabinett, and not the Trocken (dry) style of Riesling that is currently trendier in Europe? If you want dry white wine, there are dozens and dozens of other choices. Only a small handful of grape varieties can make beautiful wines with residual sugar, and Riesling is the very best of them.

That light sweetness ups the pairing ante, complementing a whole host of foods that can otherwise be devilishly difficult. There is a sweet-and-spicy

17

alchemy created when alternating sips of Riesling with a kung pao chicken or a Thai panang curry or an Indian vindaloo. The sugar helps to tame the heat. The heat electrifies the purity of the sugary fruit. It's mouth magic. Drink all those dry whites during the other eleven months of the year. In the dark gloom of February, the valentines among us would do well to consider Riesling. Why gift the box of chocolates and the bottle of red, when you can combine the sugar and the booze in one package?

Or stash a bottle away for a few years, and you might begin to see those Riesling minerals transform into smoky, earthy aromatics often described as "petrol." Yes, gasoline, filtered through Euro-speak. Some wine lovers adore this aroma, seeing it as a compelling grace note. Others prefer to drink their Rieslings young and save the gasoline huffing for other aspects of their personal lives.

Chilean Carménère

We all get into wine ruts. And Cabernet Sauvignon ruts must be among the deepest. In midwinter, with heavier foods abounding, there's a strong tendency to go with the tried and the true, to grab a Cab every time a rib eye or a New York strip hits the cast-iron skillet. There is a way out of this particular wine rut, via the rustic pleasure of Chilean Carménère.

Carménère serves as a particularly good Cabernet rut-buster because it shares much of Cab's textural qualities of full body and robust tannins. Tannins occur naturally in the skins and seeds of grapes (oak barrels too), and they're excellent at pulling fats and lipids off your palate. That's why wines like Cabs and Carménères are so good with a rib eye: they scrape that delicious beef tallow off your cheeks and gums, allowing each subsequent bite of steak to taste, well, steakier.

Texture is where the Cabernet/Carménère similarities end. The flavor profiles are quite different. Carménère has a wonderful savory edge that expresses itself through notes of roasted herbs and tomatoes

CHILEAN CARMÉNÈRE

WHAT	Dry red wine made from the grape variety Carménère
WHERE	Chile
WHY	The mythical lost sixth grape of Bordeaux makes for a value alternative to Cabernet Sauvignon in its adopted South American home.
PRONUNCIATION	*KAR-men-yehr*
HOW MUCH	Decent examples cost $10 to $20.
PAIR WITH	Braised short ribs, cooked long and low until spoon-tender

and smoldering leaves. Slow-braising some tough cut of meat to fork-tenderness in a mix of Carménère, herbs, and tomato paste is my ideal way to spend a February Sunday, and if a drop or two eludes the braising pot and slips into a glass, well, Sunday is still technically the weekend.

Chile is the modern home of Carménère, but its older origins are in Bordeaux. While wine enthusiasts often refer to the five red grapes of Bordeaux (Cabernet Sauvignon, Merlot, Cabernet Franc, Malbec, Petit Verdot), Carménère is the mythical lost sixth grape of the region. It was prominent in the 1800s, but after the scourge of phylloxera (a terrible sap-sucking insect) decimated Bordeaux vineyards, few growers replanted Carménère. The grape was a notorious pain in the ass to farm, susceptible to fungus and mildew and wanting way more heat than chilly Bordeaux could offer in a normal growing season.

In a different manner, Carménère was also the lost grape of Chile. For generations, Chilean winemakers had noticed that some of their Merlot vines were outliers that would ripen two or three weeks later than the rest. Then, in 1994, a French ampelographer (grape geneticist; yes, this is a real job) named Jean-Michel Boursiquot was walking a "Merlot" block in a Chilean vineyard when he noticed that the "Merlot" didn't look like Merlot. He suspected it was Carménère, and DNA testing later proved him right.

Nearly overnight, a wine industry was transformed. Thousands of acres thought to be planted to Merlot were actually planted to Carménère, and Chile instantly became the world capital of Carménère production. They have since embraced that role, labeling and exporting thousands of bottles of this characterful red.

You can learn a lot about a winery's priorities from the font size on their labels. Walk into your nearest wine retailer or grocery store, and you'll notice a curious phenomenon. Most of the wines from the New World (wine-speak for anyplace outside of Europe: regions like the United States, Australia, Chile) emphasize the grape variety. You'll see Cabernet Sauvignon emblazoned in 40-point font, and then Napa Valley or Coonawarra or Colchagua Valley in 14 point. European wines, on the other hand, shout out the place where the wine comes from and whisper the grapes, if they mention varieties at all. Why is this the case?

It's mostly related to timescale. European viticulture dates back thousands of years, beginning with Roman expansion in the first centuries AD. What happened throughout subsequent dozens of generations, and via what I imagine to be a lot of jolly drunken trial and error, is that European growers learned which grape varieties grew well in which particular regions and, even within regions, which particular slope or hillside produced the very best, most distinctive wines. They often codified those places with legal boundaries and winemaking rules meant to ensure consistent quality. Examples include *appellation d'origine contrôlée* (France),

denominazione di origine controllata (Italy), and *denominación de origen* (Spain). Each of these systems is used to describe demarcated regions and specific winemaking practices in those regions. Over time, with these strict guidelines set into law, place came to mean more than grape. Tempranillo wasn't so important, but Gran Reserva Rioja—that was an assurance of quality.

Instead of being measured in thousands of years, New World viticulture is on a scale closer to hundreds, or maybe dozens. It's still a grand experiment, determining which grapes are suitable for which sites. During this experimentation phase, place doesn't hold as much meaning, so the grape is emphasized. The goal of both camps is the same: to convey as honestly as possible what style a consumer should expect when opening up a bottle of wine.

Ultimately, the two paths are converging. As New World regions mature, wineries are more apt to highlight the place where their grapes are grown (think Napa Valley). And European wineries— chasing non-European export markets and customers who prefer more information— are agitating to loosen labeling laws so they can at least print varieties on the back label, if not right up front.

LAST YEAR'S ROSÉ

WHAT	Dry Rosé made from any number of grape varieties, from a vintage dated two years prior to the current calendar year
WHERE	Anywhere in the world
WHY	Panicked winemakers offer screaming deals on last year's unsold Rosés, which are often just as delicious as the current vintage.
PRONUNCIATION	*ro-ZAY*
HOW MUCH	Decent examples cost $5 to $15.
PAIR WITH	Weekend brunch: cheesy eggs, French toast, simple side salad

Last Year's Rosé

One way we can seek value is to push back against widely held beliefs about wine. Especially those that happen not to be true. Allow me to introduce you to one such belief: that Rosés have an expiration date set to December 31 of the year following harvest. This is a persistent belief in part because it contains a kernel of truth. Terrible Rosés do indeed expire quickly, and up until recently, there were a lot of terrible Rosés on the market. But we're riding the crest of a Rosé movement, and the quality has never been higher. Good, purpose-built Rosés with bright, acidic spines—those can age just like white wines, which means an extra year or two of bottle age will barely budge the needle.

To understand why there is such value in Rosés with an extra year in bottle, let's place ourselves in the calendars, and minds, of Rosé producers and importers:

April: Confidence abounds. Just as the weather is warming up, we're ready to release our Rosé made from grapes harvested last October.

July: Height of summer. Peak Rosé season. Sales have increased each month, but, hmmm . . . there are a lot of other Rosés on the market, and at this pace, we're not going to sell through our entire stash this summer.

September: Beads of sweat forming on brows. Damn, that unseasonal cold snap in August didn't help with Rosé sales. And now kids are back in school; people are thinking about autumn. Nobody's buying Rosé. But that's okay; people always drink Rosé at Thanksgiving. We'll offer a little discount and blast through the rest of this pink goodness. In the meantime, let's harvest next year's grapes!

December: Full-on flop sweat. Oh shit. Turns out some of our competitors, who have been down this road before, offered *more* than a little discount. Their Rosés hit copious Thanksgiving tables; our Rosé sales are stagnant, and we're still sitting on two hundred cases.

February: Palpitations. Rosé was supposed to be our cash-flow play, and now it's turning into a balance-sheet anchor. The new vintage of Rosé is going to be bottled in like two months. What the hell are we going to do with last year's?

Do you know what they're going to do with last year's vintage? They're going to dump it for dimes on the dollar. And that's how, in months like January and February and March, Rosés that used to cost $20 now cost $10 and Rosés that used to cost $15 now cost $5. Has the quality plummeted by 60 percent? No, it has not. Only the price.

Purchase these Rosés in February and hold them until the warmer-weather months, if you like. Or pop a few bottles in the fridge and see if you don't end up choosing one for a midweek meal. Even in midwinter, Rosé's food-pairing versatility shines through. A bracing Rosé dazzles with a roast chicken, cutting through butter-and-thyme crisped skin. Or drink it with Saturday French toast; you can upgrade to the fancy Vermont maple syrup with the money you saved on your Rosé.

ZEN PRACTICE

The research on pregnancy cravings is mixed. Some evidence points toward hormonal underpinnings, some toward psychological, some cultural. And if you think that I, as a man—a man whose closest analog to childbearing was a kidney stone, where the pregnancy was short, the labor-and-delivery excruciating, the baby unattractive, and the only craving for more Dilaudid—am going to offer an opinion on this topic, you're sorely mistaken.

What I will say is that throughout much of my wife's second pregnancy, she craved one specific food. Nachos. And so cooking nachos once each week (conservative estimate) became my Zen practice (if a Zen practice can include copious amounts of melted cheese). Every element was considered, tested, settled.

Round tortilla chips or triangles? Save the circles for your banal salsa dipping. Triangles, with their three sharp angles that emerge from a pile of nachos like whitecaps on a choppy sea, offer the perfect fingerholds.

The right meat? I started with plain ground beef. Too boring. Then I moved to ground beef with taco seasoning, which was attractive in the same way that a salt lick must be attractive to deer. I tried carnitas, which tasted great but quadrupled the overall cooking time. And I settled on fresh chorizo, which offers flavor intensity, nuanced spiciness, and porky umami goodness.

For cheese, I mostly stayed in the tried-and-true melty lanes of cheddar and jack. Either on its own is flawed: the cheddar too greasy, the jack too staid. The perfect blend, in my experience: two parts jack to one part cheddar.

Because this recipe was developed with a gestating baby in mind, I was also eager to introduce a few healthier elements. Black beans were an easy call, their earthy flavor and textural snap complementing the chorizo beautifully. Lacinato kale added a bitter counterpoint to all the richness, and a pleasing crunch.

For years, my favorite nacho topper has been pickled raisins from Seattle chef Renee Erickson's Boat Street Pickles. If nachos have a weakness (blasphemy, I know), it's that they can be a little one note. The first bite tastes great, but then it's all salt-fat-umami, over and over again. Pickled raisins break the cycle. They're little acid-sugar balloons, and when they pop, the balance is enough to make women swollen with child—and their partners swollen with the kind of gallantry that only repetitive nacho cookery can provide—swoon with pleasure.

Pregnancy Nachos

Think of this more as a template for nacho goodness than a strict recipe. This particular version is meant for a quick weeknight turnaround, but if you're cooking on the weekend, you can soak dried beans instead of using canned and take your time making carnitas instead of using chorizo.

When it comes to chorizo, make sure you're working with the freshly ground Mexican sausage, not the dried Spanish variety. I love lacinato kale, not only for its flavor but also for its ease. Because the stems and leaves are all edible, prepping this type of kale is simple, with quick slices all the way across. One area where I cannot abide a shortcut is cheese. The double-melt method (one layer melted on the chips; the other layer melted on top of the toppings) is essential for optimal coverage.

Makes 4 servings

2 tablespoons unsalted butter

½ medium yellow onion, diced

1 pound fresh Mexican chorizo

½ pound lacinato kale, sliced into ½-inch-thick ribbons

¼ cup water

Kosher salt

1 (12-ounce) bag tortilla chips

1 cup grated cheddar cheese

2 cups grated jack cheese

2 cups Gussied-Up Black Beans (recipe follows)

Sour cream, for garnish

Chopped fresh cilantro, for garnish

½ cup Quick-Pickled Raisins (recipe follows), for garnish

Prepare the chorizo. Preheat the oven to 350 degrees F. In a large skillet over medium-high heat, melt the butter. Add the onion and cook until beginning to soften, about 3 minutes. Add the chorizo and continue until it's cooked through and beginning to brown, about 5 minutes. Depending on the fat content of the chorizo, the grease in the pan might be excessive at this point. If so, drain to your liking, then add the kale and cook until it begins to wilt, just another 1 to 2 minutes. Add the water, partially cover the pan, and cook until the water boils off entirely. Season with salt to taste. Cover, reduce the heat to low, and keep the mixture warm.

Assemble the nachos. Arrange the tortilla chips on a rimmed baking sheet in one single layer. Mix the two cheeses together in a medium bowl, and sprinkle half the cheese mixture evenly over the chips. Bake until the cheese just begins to melt, 5 to 10 minutes. Remove the pan from the oven, and layer with the beans, the chorizo mixture, and finally the rest of the cheese. Bake again until the cheese just begins to melt, another 5 to 10 minutes.

Serve. Channeling your inner Jackson Pollock, spoon-paint the sour cream across the nachos. Then carefully dot the nachos with cilantro and pickled raisins, opting for maximal coverage without looking too compulsive. Place the hot baking sheet right on the table, and let the people eating for two fight it out with the people eating for one. ▶

Gussied-Up Black Beans

Here we're using something similar to a Cuban-style sofrito (plus jalapeño) to gussy up a humble old can of black beans. The extra wrist effort (it's a lot of fine chopping) offers considerable flavor rewards. (Note: You could, instead of chopping, use a few pulses on a food processor, if you have one handy.)

Makes 2 cups

¼ cup extra-virgin olive oil

1 medium green bell pepper, stemmed, seeded, and finely chopped

½ medium yellow onion, finely chopped

6 cloves garlic, finely chopped

1 jalapeño pepper, stemmed, seeded, and finely chopped

Kosher salt

1 (15-ounce) can black beans, rinsed and drained

½ cup chicken stock

Make the sofrito. In a large skillet over medium heat, heat the olive oil. Add the bell pepper, onion, garlic, and jalapeño, along with a pinch of salt, and cook, stirring occasionally, until the vegetables are soft and beginning to darken, 15 to 20 minutes.

Gussy up the beans. Add the beans and stock, reduce the heat to maintain a simmer, and simmer until the beans are just warmed through and beginning to soften. Season with salt to taste. Keep the beans warm over low heat until you assemble the nachos.

Quick-Pickled Raisins

If you can't source Boat Street Pickles' inspired pickled raisins, you can always quick-pickle your own. In addition to upending nacho calculus, these little beauties are wonderful as part of a cheese plate or paired with pâté, cutting through the richness inherent to both. These can be stored in the refrigerator for up to a week.

Makes 1 cup

⅔ cup water

⅓ cup apple cider
  vinegar

¼ cup sugar

1 teaspoon whole
  mustard seeds

Pinch of kosher salt

1 cup golden raisins

Pickle the raisins. In a medium saucepan, combine the water, vinegar, sugar, mustard seeds, and salt. Bring to a boil over medium-high heat, stirring occasionally, then reduce the heat to maintain a strong simmer. Simmer until the sugar is dissolved and the liquid has reduced by about a third, 10 to 20 minutes. Add the raisins and stir well. Return to a simmer briefly (about 1 minute), then remove from the heat.

Substitutions and Notes: Because the beans and raisins each take some time, consider making both of those before sautéing the chorizo. If you can't find Mexican chorizo, consider substituting fresh ground pork seasoned with salt, paprika, and cumin. Any kale will do if lacinato is unavailable; Swiss chard also works great as a substitute.

Pairing: While a crisp Rosé has the acidity to cut through the cheesy nachos, and a Carménère the ability to underscore the spicy notes of the chorizo, my first-choice wine is Mosel Riesling, which has just as much acid as the Rosé but also a touch of sweetness to balance the porky/salty umami of the nachos. It serves the same role in liquid form that the pickled raisins serve in solid form.

HUNTER VALLEY SÉMILLON

WHAT	Dry white wine made from the grape variety Sémillon
WHERE	Hunter Valley, just north of Sydney in New South Wales, Australia
WHY	This is a low-alcohol, rippin'-acid white perfect for springtime, and one that ages in fascinating directions with a few years in bottle.
PRONUNCIATION	*say-meel-YOHNG*
HOW MUCH	Decent examples cost $15 to $30.
PAIR WITH	Simple seared scallops or other delicate seafood

Hunter Valley Sémillon

Hunter Valley Sémillon makes no sense. It's a freak. Like *Purple Rain*–era Prince freaky. Take Sémillon, a white grape notoriously low in natural acidity. Plant it in a scorching-hot valley north of Sydney. Warm regions generally produce super-ripe grapes: high sugars, low acids. You'd expect the wine to be a hot, flabby mess: some 15-percent-alcohol booze-monster entirely lacking in energy and charm. What you get is the opposite: a brisk beauty that dazzles in its youth and gathers nuance and complexity with age.

In its resplendent youth, Hunter Valley Sémillon seems built for early spring, green shoots pushing up through frozen soil, announcing the end of winter's dominion. Out of necessity—due to the warmth of the region and a rainy season that begins early—winemakers in the valley have to pick their Sémillon extremely early, with grape sugars still quite low. The resulting wine ends up bone dry, with tooth-rattling acidity, alcohol levels in the 9 to 11 percent range, and a compelling grassy edge, somewhere between a Sauvignon Blanc and a fine herbal gin, to go with piercing purity of limey fruit.

Part of what makes Hunter Valley Sémillon special is what happens with bottle age. Over time (starting at about three years past vintage, and evolving until maybe fifteen to twenty years) the acidity softens, the color darkens, and the fresh grass notes turn to savory hay and straw. Oddest of all: a distinctive nutty/toasty note emerges, mimicking oak influence in wines that were raised entirely in stainless steel.

From its beginning, this has been a region of contradictions. The Hunter Valley was originally planted to grapevines with governmental encouragement, for the purposes of public sobriety. Let that sink in for a moment. Planting wine grapes to encourage sobriety. Questionable strategy? Not when you consider who settled New South Wales (the original landing party in 1788 was 55 percent British convicts) and what the beverage of choice was in those days (high-octane spirits). By comparison, wine seemed civilized.

To give a sense of how historically intertwined viticulture is with this region: vineyards arrived before roads. By 1823, dozens of acres of vineyards were planted in the valley. The first roads (built by convicts, naturally) didn't arrive until the early 1830s. Since then, those roads have carried many a Sydneysider up into wine country. And that presents one of the challenges of Hunter Valley Sémillon: it is gobbled up in great quantities by residents of Sydney, only a two-hour drive away. A modest amount of wine is set aside for export, and a small fraction of that makes its way to the United States. Still, discerning retailers and restaurateurs will go out of their way to feature Hunter Valley Sémillon; it is one of the world's truly distinctive wines.

Brézème Rouge

The Syrahs of the Northern Rhône are among the most coveted wines in the world. And the most expensive. Regions like Côte-Rôtie and Hermitage have long dazzled wine lovers with their wines' aromatic profiles, which possess as many nonfruit elements as fruits. Bacon fat and smoked sausages, briny green olives and seaweed, flowers and minerals and soil: all notes that turn up in descriptions of Syrah from this part of the world. Those of us with a taste for the umami, for the savory, cannot get enough of these wines.

Let's leave Côte-Rôtie and Hermitage to the trust-fund set and drink Brézème, in the southern hinterlands of the Northern Rhône. Brézème is still obscure, still difficult to source. There are only a handful of wineries working in the region, and only a plurality of those are exported. Persevere. Seek these wines out. They offer foie-gras quality on a scrapple budget. And they won't always be this inexpensive. The wineries in this region have long agitated for full status as an independent appellation (right now they have to be labeled "Brézème–Côtes du Rhône" or "Côtes du Rhône–Brézème"), which would put them on par with regions like Côte-Rôtie and Hermitage and would set them on an inevitable course toward stratospheric pricing.

BRÉZÈME ROUGE

WHAT	Dry red wine made from the grape variety Syrah
WHERE	The Northern Rhône Valley in France
WHY	An obscure appellation in the Northern Rhône is producing savory, meaty Syrahs to rival its more prestigious (and expensive) neighbors.
PRONUNCIATION	*bray-ZEM roozh*
HOW MUCH	Decent examples cost $20 to $30.
PAIR WITH	Lamb chops, leg of lamb, lamb shanks; basically any edible part of the lamb

DOMESTIC ROSÉ

WHAT	Dry Rosé wine made from any number of grape varieties
WHERE	The United States of America
WHY	Our country is in the midst of a Rosé revolution, and the quality has never been better.
PRONUNCIATION	*ro-ZAY*
HOW MUCH	Decent examples cost $10 to $20.
PAIR WITH	Roast chicken, the skin butter-crispy and redolent of thyme

They might succeed. In Brézème, the question has never been about quality; in fact, there was a time when Brézème wines commanded the same prices as Hermitage. That time was the mid-1800s. But then a series of devastating events: Brézème vineyards, like much of France, were ravaged by phylloxera, a truly heinous vine sap–sucking insect. Replanting vineyards took manpower, and World War I robbed the region of many of its men. The farmers of the area decided that lower-cost, higher-consistency stone fruits were the better way to go, and by the mid-twentieth century, there were far more peach and cherry orchards than vineyards in Brézème.

Recent decades have seen the stirrings of a renaissance, as intrepid winemakers priced out of vineyard land farther north have traveled to the southern reaches of the Northern Rhône. What they've found in Brézème is a unique region, one combining the chilly climate of the north with the limestone-heavy geology of the Southern Rhône. The resulting wines pair the power and palate-oomph of the south with the energy and bright acidity of the north. Brézème Syrah is a tweener wine for a tweener month, straddling styles the way March straddles winter and spring, and with all the savory complexities that have burnished Syrah's reputation in this part of the world.

Domestic Rosé

Here's how American Rosé used to work: Cabernet Sauvignon grapes, Merlot grapes, Zinfandel grapes, just about any red grapes, really, come into the winery after harvest. The grapes are stemmed and crushed, and then, after a short period—hours or maybe days, not weeks—grape juice is siphoned off from the fermentation bin before fermentation kicks off. The siphoned juice is pink, not red, because the liquid has only had a short period of time to steep on the grape skins, which contain all the color compounds.

The pink juice is bursting with sugar. Because these grapes were picked for red wines, they have red wine levels of potential alcohol contained in all that sugar: 13 or 14 or 15 percent if all the sugar is fermented into alcohol. That's a problem, because most of us like our Rosés crisp and refreshing. At this point, the winemaker is faced with an unattractive choice.

Choice one is to leave some of the sugar unfermented—to keep it as residual sugar. That's how you end up with the kind of sticky-sweet "White Zinfandels" that I drank from my parents' basement freezer in my youth. Choice two is to add water. This will lower the alcohol, but it has twin side effects, diluting flavor and muting natural acidity. Not much to be done about flavor dilution, but acidity can be adjusted by adding powdered tartaric acid. At this point, the wine is indeed a dry Rosé at 11 or 12 percent alcohol, but it's more Franken-wine than wine.

This method for Rosé-making is called *saignée*, French for "bleeding," which refers to the step where winemakers bleed juice out of their fermentation bins. *Saignée* is attractive because it concentrates the remaining juice in those bins, adding oomph to the resulting red wines, and because it turns juice that would otherwise have gone down the winery drain into quick cash flow. No surprise, though: a wine that is essentially an afterthought does not turn out to be very good.

What we've seen in the United States over the past decade is nothing short of a Rosé revolution, with winemakers eschewing the *saignée* method in favor of purpose-built Rosés. What I mean by *purpose-built* is: starting in the vineyards, these grapes and wines are designed to make light, bright, refreshing pink wines. Certain vines are designated for Rosé, and grapes from those vines are picked several weeks earlier than the red wine harvest, early enough that potential alcohols are low and acidity is high. There will be no need to add water, no need to add powdered acid, no need to leave residual sugar. The resulting wines will be pale pink or salmon colored, with berry and citrus fruits, sometimes minerality, sometimes refreshing green notes like cucumber or watermelon rind.

Rosés can be made from any red variety (and even a few "whites," like Pinot Gris), but thin-skinned grapes work best. Pinot Noir Rosés from Oregon fit the bill. So too California and Washington versions made from Grenache or Mourvèdre or Cinsault.

For those of us who adore crisp, light, bone-dry Rosé, this particular American revolution has been a boon, not least because it adds several months to Rosé-drinking season. Formerly, to access this style of Rosé, you had to wait until the container ship arrived from Provence (capital of European Rosé). Take a February or March bottling in Europe and add several months for overseas shipping, and it was the height of summer before we could have our first Rosé breakfast. Now that domestic wineries are making this style, we can take that same February or March bottling and add about five minutes before the wines are ready to chill and glug with cheesy scrambled eggs.

March Meal

Braised Lamb Shanks with Cabbage Raab and Garlicky White Beans

A GREEN OF MANY NAMES

I remember vividly the first time I saw a "cabbage raab." We were on a late-March vacation, my family and I, chasing sunshine after a long winter. Our rental cottage was within walking distance of a little farmstand, and I ambled over there with notions of a root vegetable gratin floating around the dinner-planning part of my brain. I expected to see turnips and carrots, rutabagas and potatoes, and I did. But then, out of the corner of my eye, a bolt of green. I was drawn to it like a scurvy patient to a lemon tree. Depravation as motivation.

After all, by late March it had been months since I had seen anything fresh and green at a farmers' market. The only fresh veggies were root veggies. The only green veggies were pickled or canned. Not that there's anything wrong with that! I love a pickled green bean as much as the next guy, but after months of preserved foods, a body cries out for something a little more photosynthetic.

This cranny of the farmstand had a whole collection of greens. Kale raabs and mustard raabs. Brussels sprout raabs and collard raabs. But none drew my eye quite like the cabbage raabs, which looked like red and green leafy microphones. The lone farmstand worker, sympathetic to my fugue state, encouraged me to try one—raw. Conditioned by many a meal of rapini (often confusingly called *broccoli raab*, even though it is not technically the raab of broccoli), I was expecting the height of bitterness. Turns out this was a different raab entirely.

What I tasted wasn't bitter at all. It was sweet, earthy, and intensely green, with a flavor like the echo of cabbage shouted between canyon walls. I was transfixed. I bought all the raabs I could find and spent the weekend sautéing, grilling, and braising them into every meal I could think of. Yes, breakfast too: chopped cabbage raab folded into eggs scrambled with Boursin cheese. It felt like a spring accelerant. Like cheating. Like lining up for a race, then getting away with a false start that the judges didn't catch.

In between meals, I spent time on the culinary back roads of the internet, reading everything I could about these greens. Turns out they are specific to one genus of vegetable: *Brassica*, the group that contains broccoli and cauliflower, cabbages and brussels sprouts, kales and mustard greens. The raabs are the flowering heads of overwintered brassica. Also turns out they have more aliases than a capable spy. I saw cabbage raab variously referred to as cabbage shoots, cabbage sprouts, cabbage buds, cabbage flowers, cabbage tops, and cabbage heads. (Great band names one and all.)

At some point, we're all going to settle on one name for these green gems, and then their popularity is going to explode. These raab-shoot-sprout-bud-flower-top-heads have already become trendy at farmers' markets, and I can understand why. It's not just that they're delicious; they also extend green-veggie season considerably, outpacing early asparagus by nearly a month. For those of us with a drug-like relationship to food, this is exactly the spring fix we've been craving.

Braised Lamb Shanks
with Cabbage Raab and Garlicky White Beans

You really want to feature the raab in this meal, so give each diner just one lamb shank: protein as supporting actor. Traditionally, many sheep farmers aimed for late-winter-birthed lambs that could be moved directly from mother's milk to the tender grass shoots of early spring. That timing underpins the idea of lamb as a spring food. Here we take a tough, intensely flavored (but not as gamey as some other parts) cut of lamb—the shank—and slow-cook it until it gives way to hungry forks. Continuing our green theme, we'll use for our braising vegetables celery and leeks, the grassiest allium.

Makes 4 servings

1 tablespoon unsalted butter	½ head celery, roughly chopped, leaves reserved for garnish	Garlicky White Beans (recipe follows)
1 tablespoon extra-virgin olive oil	1 large leek, white and light-green parts only, washed and roughly chopped	Cabbage Raab with Lemony Bread Crumbs (recipe follows)
4 medium lamb shanks (3 to 4 pounds total)	1 cup dry white wine, plus more as needed	
Kosher salt		

Sear the shanks. Preheat the oven to 300 degrees F. In a large braising pot over medium-high heat, melt the butter and olive oil together. Season the shanks on all sides with salt, then add the shanks to the pot and brown on all sides, about 3 minutes per side, or 12 minutes total. If all four shanks won't fit, brown them in two batches. Set the shanks aside.

Prepare the braise. Add the celery and leek to the pot and sauté until beginning to soften, 6 to 8 minutes. Add the wine and deglaze, scraping any browned bits from the bottom of the pot. Bring to a boil. ▶

Braise the shanks. Place the shanks on top of the veggies, cover the pot, and place in the oven. Cook for about 3 hours, turning the shanks every 45 minutes and checking on the braising liquid. If it gets close to evaporating entirely, add another ½ cup wine. The shanks are finished when the tongs you use to turn them start accidentally pulling the meat off the bone.

Serve. I prefer a rustic presentation here. Spoon the garlicky beans into the bottom of four wide bowls, and top with ribbons of cabbage raab and one whole lamb shank. Chop the reserved celery leaves and garnish each serving.

Garlicky White Beans

This time of year, you might be lucky enough to find green garlic at your farmers' market. This is just young garlic, before it has formed proper bulbs. If you do get your hands on some, substitute four stalks for the four cloves of garlic; it'll add grassy subtleties to the garlicky beans.

Makes 4 servings

¼ cup extra-virgin olive oil

½ head celery, finely chopped

1 large leek, white and light-green parts only, washed and finely chopped

4 cloves garlic, finely chopped

Kosher salt

½ cup dry white wine

2 (15-ounce) cans cannellini beans, drained and rinsed

Juice from 1 medium lemon

Sauté the vegetables. In a large skillet over medium heat, heat the olive oil. Add the celery, leek, and garlic, along with a pinch of salt, and cook, stirring occasionally, until the vegetables are soft, about 10 minutes.

Simmer the beans. Add the wine and deglaze, scraping any browned bits from the bottom of the skillet. Bring to a gentle boil until the wine is almost completely evaporated. Add the beans, lower the heat to maintain a simmer, and simmer until the beans are just warmed through and beginning to soften. Season with lemon juice and more salt to taste. Keep warm over low heat until ready to serve.

Cabbage Raab with Lemony Bread Crumbs

Cabbage greens respond well to all sorts of preparations. Perhaps tomorrow we'll throw a few on the grill and enjoy the resulting char and crunch. But for the first raab of the year, we want to freebase the green. A simple blanch works best. For minimal waste, and maximum textural interest, use the entire plant: stems, leaves, and flowers.

Makes 4 servings

2 tablespoons unsalted butter

½ cup panko bread crumbs

Zest and juice from 1 medium lemon, zest very finely minced

1½ pounds cabbage raab, roughly chopped

Prepare the bread crumbs. In a medium skillet over medium heat, melt the butter and stir in the panko. Sauté until just beginning to brown, then stir in the lemon zest, cook for 30 more seconds, and set aside.

Prepare the raab. In a large saucepan, bring 2 quarts of salted water to a boil. Add the raab and cook until crisp-tender—start checking at 1 minute; it should take no more than 3 minutes. Drain, and top first with the lemon juice, then with the bread crumbs.

Substitutions and Notes: The season for raabs is a short one, maybe a month at best. For the remainder of the year, the closest vegetable in terms of texture is Broccolini, and it makes a fine raab substitute. If you can't find lamb shanks, any tough cut of red meat will do: short ribs, oxtails, veal shanks, even pot roast. Regular bread crumbs are fine if panko is not available; so too navy beans in place of cannellini.

Pairing: Syrah is the traditional lamb pairing, but Brézème may be a little bold for the other components on the plate. Likewise, Hunter Valley Sémillon would work for the raab and beans, but its flavors are a bit delicate for the lamb. A domestic Rosé is the Goldilocks bottle, with enough richness and weight to stand up to the lamb and the delicacy to match nicely with the raab and beans.

How to Enjoy Wine with Food

Tell me if this scene sounds familiar. You go out to dinner and order a bottle of wine. The wine arrives, glasses are poured, cheers, and glug-glug-glug along with fascinating conversation. Now the food arrives, and the wine stem is moved aside to make way for the plates. Oh, man, this steak/burrito/curry is delicious! Food, food, food; talk, talk, talk. And suddenly you've cleared your plate; time to return to the wineglass.

Is there anything wrong with this scenario? Objectively, no. This is dinner-as-dinner and wine-as-aperitif-and-digestif. But it is not food-and-wine pairing.

In order to actually experience the alchemical beauty of food and wine together, you have to, ya know, have the food and wine together. Overly simplistic? Perhaps, but I've lost track of the number of dinner guests I've watched drink some wine, then eat all the food, then drink some more wine.

In the interests of better pairing, I present this simple three-step guide. Step 1: Enjoy a sip of wine. Step 2: Enjoy a bite of food. Step 3: Repeat.

I once spoke to a dedicated cheesemonger, and she told me that her method for developing suitable wine-cheese pairings is to take a bite of the cheese, hold it in her mouth, then add a sip of wine to create a slurry. If the slurry tastes good, successful pairing! Bad taste, bad pairing. I'm not going to ask you to start making salmon–Pinot Noir slurries. (In fact, the sooner I can stop writing the word *slurry,* the better.) But I do suggest alternating bites and sips; it will enhance the experience of each.

QUINCY/REUILLY/
MENETOU-SALON

WHAT	Dry white wine made from the grape variety Sauvignon Blanc
WHERE	The eastern Loire Valley of France
WHY	Sauvignon Blanc from the Loire is grassy and delicious, and these regions offer stronger value than their better-known neighbors, Sancerre and Pouilly-Fumé.
PRONUNCIATION	*KAHN-see / ROY-yee / mehn-eh-too-sa-LOHN*
HOW MUCH	Decent examples cost $15 to $25.
PAIR WITH	Sugar snap peas, boiled for 30 seconds and lightly salted

Quincy/Reuilly/ Menetou-Salon

A crisp, grassy Sauvignon Blanc from the Loire Valley, consumed on one of those mid-April days that contains the first kernel of the warmer months to follow, ideally drunk alongside a slab of fresh goat cheese; here is one of the wine world's gifts to humanity. Springtime subsumed into liquid.

The only problem: the prices for the most famous Loire Valley Sauvignon Blancs have crept steadily up over recent years, to where a good bottle of Sancerre or Pouilly-Fumé now costs north of $30. Those wines are undeniably lovely, but when we purchase them, we're paying for quality *plus* a reputation markup. Better to seek out the regions without a robust marketing budget—regions where the reputation markup is zero.

Enter Quincy, Reuilly, and Menetou-Salon, a triumvirate of lesser-known Sauvignon Blanc freeholds in the eastern Loire. Their relative obscurity means that they're best rolled together as a threesome. You may not be able to find all three, but chances are you'll be able to find at least one. Menetou-Salon is directly adjacent to Sancerre; Quincy and Reuilly, one valley to the west. Each one is capable of the Sauvignon Blanc trinity: citrus and mineral and grass.

That last descriptor is what makes Sauvignon Blanc such a singular grape. It is the only prominent white variety to contain high levels of compounds called pyrazines, the same compounds that occur in large concentrations in bell peppers. Grapes with significant pyrazines all tend to share a green edge, and with Sauvignon Blanc, the green spectrum runs from New Zealand versions, which tend to express overt jalapeño notes, to California versions, which ripen to a level that precludes the expression of any greenness at all (simple peach fruit is more common).

Loire Sauvignon Blanc occupies a middle ground, offering aromatics suggestive of a freshly mowed lawn, where that lawn may have included a small herb garden. Those grassy notes comingle with grapefruit and stony minerals, all on a frame typically low in alcohol and high in acidity, thanks to the cool climate of this part of France.

Each of the three regions possesses unique appeal. Menetou-Salon shares the coveted limestone soil of Sancerre and produces wines that can be Sancerre ringers. Quincy has historical interest as the second-ever appellation created in France (Châteauneuf-du-Pape was the first) and produces a delicate, floral version of Sauvignon Blanc. And Reuilly is expanding the most rapidly of the three, as consumers are drawn to its more rugged, slightly fuller style.

Compared to the Sauvignon Blanc area planted in Sancerre (5,400 acres) and Pouilly-Fumé (3,000 acres), these three appellations are tiny: 800 acres for Menetou-Salon, 600 for Quincy, 500 for Reuilly. So long as they continue to operate in the shadows cast by their better-known neighbors, these regions will offer outstanding value for those of us seeking green in springtime.

Tinta de Toro

Allow me to introduce you to the unpublished second verse of a famous ditty: *In fourteen hundred and ninety-two / Columbus sailed the ocean blue / and every night before his bed / he drank a glass of Toro red.* That's right: if you drink a glass of Tinta de Toro, you may just be continuing the longest wine-drinking tradition in the Americas.

When Christopher Columbus toasted his discovery of the "East Indies" in the stateroom of the *Santa María*, he very likely did so with a glass of Tinta de Toro. Wine was safer to drink than water during this period, especially after weeks on a ship. Columbus would have sought to provision his ships with a robust red that would not easily oxidize while sloshing around in barrels set in a ship's hold in the middle of an Atlantic crossing. Tempranillo from Toro was known for two things: burly tannins and high alcohol, both of which put up protective barriers against the scourge of oxygen.

Much of what appealed to Columbus in 1492 still appeals today. Toro still offers the world its own unique shade of Tempranillo, full of dense

TINTA DE TORO

WHAT	Dry red wine made predominantly from the grape variety Tempranillo
WHERE	Western Spain, close to the Portugal border
WHY	Spain produces the finest Tempranillo in the world, and Toro presents value alternatives to the wines of Rioja and Ribera del Duero.
PRONUNCIATION	*TEEN-tah deh TOH-roh*
HOW MUCH	Decent examples cost $15 to $25.
PAIR WITH	A medium-rare New York strip steak or other beefy cut of your choosing

DOMESTIC SPARKLING WINE

WHAT	Sparkling wine made from any number of grape varieties (typically Chardonnay and/or Pinot Noir)
WHERE	The United States of America
WHY	We should all drink more sparkling wine. We have our very own burgeoning scene in the United States, and not just in traditional wine-producing states.
HOW MUCH	Decent examples cost $10 to $20.
PAIR WITH	A bucket of buttered popcorn and a good movie at home

black fruit and rustic charm, and does so at prices considerably more approachable than the twin kings of Spanish Tempranillo, Rioja and Ribera del Duero. Over the past few decades, outside investment from regions like Ribera has improved the winemaking technology in Toro, allowing the wines to keep getting better and better, while the prices remain stubbornly low.

Toro sits on a high, arid plateau of sandy soil, with grapevines as just about the only crop that can survive the blistering summers. Tinta de Toro is a clone of Tempranillo that, over time, has evolved to become perfectly suited to the harsh conditions of the region. The grapes put on thick skins and take on copious sugar ripeness over the course of a growing season. Those thick skins translate to chewy tannins in the finished wines; the sugar to hearty alcohol. Compared to Rioja, known for alcohol levels closer to 12.5 percent and more savory/leafy flavors, Toro is a generous charmer, fruit driven and delicious. Look for dense black fruit (blackberry, black cherry) complicated by notes of spice (star anise) and earth. It's a Goldilocks wine, with medium body, medium structure, medium alcohol (usually around 13.5 percent; high for Spain but moderate in a global context): just right for a transition month like April and still suitable for any voyages of discovery.

Domestic Sparkling Wine

Spring is a lovely time of year to drink sparkling wine. Though I hasten to add: so too are summer, autumn, and winter. If I could offer only one piece of advice to enhance your wine-drinking enjoyment, it would be: drink more sparkling wine. It is a category almost completely associated with special occasions, but here's the thing: if you open a bottle of sparkling wine, you've just created the special occasion.

Sparkling wine can and should be used well beyond its role in toasting all of life's major- and minor-key successes. The most often-missed aspect of bubbly is its inveterate versatility at the table. Bubbly pairs as well with breakfast as with dinner. Sparkling wine with your Saturday-morning omelet will make you a better parent to your kids all weekend long. It pairs with all sorts of not-so-easy-to-pair foods. Buttered popcorn. Potato chips. Even a salad with a vinaigrette so tangy it makes your eyes water will be no match for a proper bottle of sparkling wine.

A combination of factors makes these wines so delightful with such a wide variety of foods. There's the naturally high acidity and, of course, the bubbles, both of which combine to scrub your palate clean and ready it for the next delicious bite of food. Then there are the smoky, bready notes from aging the wine on its lees (dead yeasts).

Extended bottle aging on yeast is how sparkling wine is made in its ancestral home, Champagne. By law, only sparkling wines that come from the region of Champagne can put "Champagne" on their labels. Domestic wineries often print *"Méthode Champenoise"* on their labels, and it doesn't take a Rosetta Stone to decipher what that means. Those are the domestic wineries to seek out: the ones producing sparkling wine the same way they do it in Champagne.

The United States has a burgeoning sparkling wine scene. Each of the major West Coast wine-producing states has at least one major player. Washington has Domaine Ste. Michelle and Treveri Cellars, Oregon has Argyle Winery, and California has a history of sparkling wine dating back to the late 1800s. Multiple Champagne houses have set up satellite shops in California: Domaine Carneros, Roederer Estate, and Domaine Chandon, to name a few. The Finger Lakes region in New York has a robust sparkling wine scene as well.

And perhaps the most surprising American success story is Gruet Winery, a sparkling wine house in New Mexico of all places. Gilbert Gruet, of the Champagne house Gruet et Fils, took a trip to the United States in 1983 and returned to France intrigued by the potential in New Mexico. Intrigued enough to purchase land, plant a vineyard in 1984, and send two of his four children there. Gruet's first harvest was in 1987, resulting in enough fruit for four hundred cases of wine. Since then, they have grown to produce about one hundred thousand cases annually—a production level equal to that of Gruet et Fils, which continues in Champagne, and enough sparkling wine to pair with an awful lot of chile verde.

Why Do You Taste Like That?

Folks in the wine trade tend to taste wine a little differently. In most cases, it's for a good reason: we're trying to pay extra-careful attention to what's in our glass, to evaluate whether it should end up on or in our retail shelf/restaurant list/personal stash. Without question, this can cross the line into pretense: the exaggerated swirl, the too-deep sniff, the enraptured reaction. Ignore the grotesquerie: there are real tips to be gleaned here.

Why swirl? Wine is a changeling, and the vast majority of its changes come from exposure to oxygen. Swirling a wine in the glass introduces oxygen and agitates aromatic compounds. Try one sniff preswirl and one sniff after; the composition of the nose may not change much, but the expressiveness will invariably increase, like turning up a volume dial.

Why sniff? Smell and taste are inextricably linked. By smelling the wine, you're priming the olfactory pump for the flavors to come. And don't be shy—the best way to fully appreciate a wine's aroma is to get your honker fully into the stem.

If the tip of your nose touches the wine, you've gone too far.

Why gurgle? If you do a quick sip-and-swallow, you're using only a small fraction of the sensory receptors in your mouth. It would be like a painter restricting herself to one corner of her canvas. Gurgling is a palate-coating device meant to bring the full weight of your senses to bear on the wine. Some wine pros also like to suck in air while gurgling—again as a way to introduce oxygen to the wine. I've always found that technique distracting to me and deeply annoying to those around me, so I'm more of a wine-as-mouthwash gurgler. (Not to be confused as gargler; please don't gargle wine—that's just gross.)

Why spit? If you don't spit, you get drunk. And if you get drunk, *everything* tastes good. Okay, that sounds kinda nice, admittedly, but if you're tasting for evaluation, you want your palate—and judgment—as unadulterated as possible. Spitting is also wise if you're doing a day of winery visits. You'll be able to meaningfully try many more wines over the course of the day if you're not hammered forty minutes in.

Campfire Foil Pouches

FISHSICLE

Back before my wife and I brought our two little tax deductions into the world, who are too heavy to carry and who refuse to walk three miles in under eight-and-a-half hours, we used to celebrate the arrival of outdoors season with an April backpacking trip, alongside a bunch of childless friends equally ignorant of the shared freedom that seemed like it would abide indefinitely.

This was always a superior time to hit the trail: warm enough that our Nalgenes didn't freeze overnight, cool enough to suppress the madding crowds, and early enough that campsite reservations weren't required. Total freedom! All we needed were our tents, our legs, and our enduring love of the natural world. Oh, and camping permits, a wilderness parking pass, rain flies, a loud bear whistle, sturdy boots, accurate maps, current-year tide tables, sleeping bags, sleeping mats, maybe a small pillow, and probably some comfy shoes for chilling in camp. That's it.

Well, except for food. I'm not really the type who likes to rough it in the culinary sense. It took only a few rehydrations of dehydrated backpacking meal pouches to realize that "Chicken & Rice" was a misnomer for "Sodium & MSG" and that a little extra food weight in the pack could pay some very serious dividends at the campsite. It's a scientific fact that food tastes better when cooked and eaten around a campfire, so even modest efforts lead to disproportionate raves.

April is the month when fresh halibut first hits the market. You may think that fresh fish and backpacking do not really mix, and based on several of my experiences, you'd be right. There was the year that we all admired the sunset too much and sacrificed considerable chunks of our filets to the local crow population. There was the year that my backpack smelled like moldering fish for the remainder of outdoors season. These were teachable moments. The lesson? Fishsicle. Toss the halibut in the freezer the night before the trip. Over the course of the drive and the hike and the building of the fire, the fish thaws to ready-to-cook temperature just in time to hit the smoldering ashes.

As for wine, I'll admit it's not the most efficient alcoholic beverage by booze-to-weight standards (that would be whiskey, which you should also bring), but a crisp white chilled in a campside, glacier-fed creek, sucked down through a foot-long hose attached to a plastic bladder? That is hillbilly haute cuisine.

Potato Pouches

Where I grew up, a foil wrapper of any kind was often called a "south Philly oven," great for keeping cheesesteaks nice and melty for an hour at a time; this approach works equally well on camping trips. If you're making these in the oven at home, 30 to 40 minutes at 375 degrees F should achieve the same effect.

For the most consistent results, and the lowest chance of charring, the foil pouches should not be right in the inferno, but essentially in an ash pit surrounded by glowing embers. The perfect pouch will contain crunchy-edged fluffy golden pillows of potato along with crisp bacon bits and charred leeks.

Makes 4 servings

1 large leek, white and
    light-green parts only
4 slices bacon

1½ pounds Yukon Gold
    potatoes
4 tablespoons unsalted
    butter

Kosher salt
4 (12-by-12-inch) pieces
    aluminum foil

Prep at home. Wash and finely chop the leek. Slice the bacon into lardons/bacon "bits" (about ¼ inch). Transfer the bacon and leeks to a sealed plastic bag. Chop the potatoes into a small dice (about ¾ inch; the smaller size will help with faster cooking) and store in a separate sealed plastic bag. Slice the butter into four 1-tablespoon pieces and store in plastic wrap. Pack about 2 tablespoons salt (enough for the potato pouches and the halibut pouches).

Create the "oven." Build a blazing campfire and let it die down on its own. When it's nice and hot, with a glowing core of embers, build your oven by moving some of those glowing embers into a small ring close to the fire.

Prep the pouches. For each pouch, place potatoes in the center of a square of foil, then top with one-quarter of the bacon-leek mixture, one pat of butter, and a generous seasoning of salt. Fold all four foil edges over the food and seal as tightly as you can.

Cook the pouches. Carefully place each pouch in the makeshift oven (using tongs or sticks) and rotate the pouches occasionally as they cook. The goal is a steady sizzle, and when you begin to smell charred leek, it's time to pull the pouches; figure on 30 to 40 minutes.

Serve. Give the pouches a brief 5-minute rest away from the fire, then place each still-warm pouch on the lap of an appreciative friend. The pouch is meal and plate, all in one.

AUSTRIAN GRÜNER VELTLINER

WHAT	Dry white wine made from the grape variety Grüner Veltliner
WHERE	Austria
WHY	Grüner is a rare beast—a savory white wine—which opens it up to all sorts of fascinating pairing potential.
PRONUNCIATION	*GROO-ner FELT-lih-ner*
HOW MUCH	Decent examples cost $15 to $20.
PAIR WITH	A mustardy green lentil salad studded with shredded ham hock

Austrian Grüner Veltliner

Celery seed. Lentil. Sweet corn. Hay. These may sound more like feed-bucket components than wine-tasting notes, but they are indeed frequently apt descriptors of Austrian Grüner Veltliner. The great wine of Austria is also that rare beast: a savory white. The primary descriptors for most white wines are fruit based: tree fruits like apples and pears, stone fruits like peaches and apricots, citrus fruits like lemons and grapefruits. And don't get me wrong; Grüner does contain fruit (often peach), but it's only one component of a complex pastiche of aromas and flavors that commonly includes one or more of the aforementioned savories, not to mention a robust spiciness akin to white pepper.

Many of us who love drinking wine with food eventually find ourselves craving Grüner with regularity. Its unique flavor spectrum opens it up to pairings that can otherwise be challenging. One example: May is often the month where radishes first appear at farmers' markets, and I will happily eat a simple lunch of sliced radishes with a crusty baguette, some good olive oil, and a small pile of kosher salt. But what to drink?

Fruity whites strike a dissonant chord with the savory vegetal spice of a good radish. A green-edged Sauvignon Blanc gets closer, but Grüner is the superior choice, its subtle spice accenting the similarly restrained kick of the radish. Grüner Veltliner is perfect for springtime and all its green goodness. Not just radishes, but lettuces and fava beans and sweet peas. It's also an underrated companion to spring-run salmon, especially a robustly flavored sockeye; Grüner's midweight texture holds up well against a rich slab, and its savory notes enhance salmon's inherent minerality.

No surprise, given its food-pairing powers: Grüner established its American beachhead via restaurant wine lists, with chefs and sommeliers championing it as a Best Supporting Actor nominee when their food needs to play the starring role. In recent years, Grüners have gained momentum in the States as inexpensive, food-friendly alternatives for those of us bored with our usual white wines.

63

Rarely in the wine world are one grape and one country so deeply intertwined. More than three-quarters of all the world's Grüner comes from Austria, and Austrian Grüner's roots run deep. There is evidence of the Habsburg royalty provisioning their troops with thousands of leather wineskins filled with Grüner Veltliner during the Ottoman-Habsburg wars. And since we all took European History in sixth-grade pubescence (we had a lot on our minds), let me refresh your memory and tell you that the Ottoman-Habsburg wars took place beginning in the 1500s. That's a solid half millennium of collected knowledge on how to coax profundity from this rogue white.

Oregon Pinot Noir

Maybe it was a Cabernet Sauvignon that first set your heart aflutter; maybe it was a Malbec that helped you put aside Miller Genuine Draft for good. We wine lovers arrive at our initial affections through many means, many grapes. So why is it that when we're ready to settle down and grow old together, we always end up proposing marriage to Pinot Noir? The more wine we drink, the more we come to value subtlety. A few years into any good wine obsession, and that rich Cabernet that seemed so appealing in the early years now feels like a heavy lift. Pinot is there, waiting patiently.

It is a grape apart. Difficult where others are easy, delicate instead of forceful, and subtle in a world that favors the obvious. There's simply nothing else like Pinot Noir. To begin with, it's among the thinnest-skinned of varieties. Literally. Pinot Noir's naturally thin skins mean that the finished wines are light in color, low in tannin.

Figuratively too. Pinot is a grape that really can't handle an insult. In the vineyard, it produces tightly bunched clusters, all the individual grape berries rubbing up against each other like commuters in a packed Tokyo subway. Which means no airflow. Which means the slightest hint of humidity leads to mildews and fungi and other undesirables. Pinot also doesn't like too much heat. Grow it in a warm climate, and it produces

OREGON PINOT NOIR

WHAT	Dry red wine made from the grape variety Pinot Noir
WHERE	Oregon, preferably from the Willamette Valley or one of its sub-appellations
WHY	There's nothing in the world quite like ethereal Pinot Noir, and Oregon produces Pinots priced more accessibly than their Burgundian counterparts.
PRONUNCIATION	*pee-noh nwahr*
HOW MUCH	Decent examples cost $20 to $40.
PAIR WITH	Wild mushroom risotto, especially if you can find morels

insipid nothingburgers that have as much in common with proper Pinot Noir as a sunflower has with the sun.

Why put up with all this angst? For the same reason we put up with angst-ridden teenagers: the potential that they'll blossom into something special. Special Pinot Noir dazzles with its subtlety. Because its fruit characteristics are not overt, it is nakedly expressive of where it is grown. And there are only a tiny handful of regions on earth where Pinot Noir can thrive. Even *thrive* is probably too strong a word. The regions where Pinot Noir does best are all marginal climates, where in maybe one of five years you get a really easy growing season, and the other four feature rain or hail or bunch rot or aggressive birds.

Burgundy is Pinot's ancestral homeland, with monks making famous wines as early as the Middle Ages, and with evidence of Pinot being cultivated in the area for another thousand years before that. That's a long time for Burgundian winemakers to hone their marketing message, and they've done so successfully, pushing the market for Burgundy Pinot Noir to stratospheric levels. That means we in the 99 percent need to find non-ancestral-homeland sources for our Pinot Noir, and one of the very best is Oregon.

The Oregon Pinot movement began in the 1960s, when several enterprising graduates of America's finest wine program (University of California, Davis) ventured north, betting that Oregon had just the right kind of garbage climate Pinot Noir would love. But it wasn't until 1980 that the landscape shifted seismically. That was the year Burgundian scion Robert Drouhin included an Oregon Pinot (the 1975 Eyrie Vineyards South Block Reserve Pinot Noir) in a blind tasting against many of Maison Joseph Drouhin's finest Burgundies. Finishing in first place: one of Drouhin's 1959 Pinots; and in second, two-tenths of a point behind: Eyrie.

That event set in motion the eventual move by Drouhin to establish an Oregon outpost, which they did with the establishment of Domaine Drouhin Oregon in 1987. The region has been on fire since, producing Pinot Noir with succulent red and black fruit, and with an appealing earthiness less like Burgundian minerality and more like Oregon's coastal rainforest floors. A resinous red-fruited Oregon Pinot with a slab of spring-run Pacific salmon? Gustatory glory.

Among the many ways we wine lovers tie ourselves into mental knots is decision-making around stemware. I have no problem with different glasses for every occasion. Flutes, goblets, jam jars—all fine by me. But if you want to simplify and declutter, you can choose one reliable type of stem, buy a dozen of them, and use them to serve every single wine you drink. Just keep in mind the four important *S*'s of stemware:

Size. Choose a stem that's too small, and you'll end up swirling wine right out of the glass and onto your white shirt. (It's an unfortunate reality that wine spills only happen while wearing light colors.) Choose one that's too big, and you'll need to pour half the bottle to even have a chance to access the wine's aromas. Goldilocks size runs about 12 to 18 ounces.

Shape. Proportionally, you want a bowl shaped more like a *U* than like a sideways *C* (unless you mostly drink high-end Burgundy, in which case go with the wider bowl, and congrats on your trust fund). Look for a bowl that broadens out near the stem, then tapers gently toward the top of the glass. That tapering will facilitate nonspill swirling, and it will concentrate aromas.

Stem. I'll admit: I like the rustic, casual look of a stemless wineglass. However, unless you're cold-blooded as a White Walker, you're going to have a problem, and that problem is hand heat. Your hand is warm right now, which I acknowledge as I read it back sounds like a creepy pickup line, but this is merely a fact of human nature. Those sweaty palms of yours are going to rapidly warm up your wine, ruining all your efforts to serve your bottle at the perfect temperature. Purchase glasses with stems.

Safety. Fear not: wineglasses are not inherently dangerous. I'm talking about dishwasher safety. The reason I think it's important to purchase dishwasher-safe glasses? Because you'll drink more wine that way. And then you'll be a happier person. You and I both harbor secret grudges against all the non-dishwasher-safe items in our kitchen. They languish in the sink for days until we've run out of cat videos to browse, and only then do we grumpily reach for the dish soap.

So there you have it: buy medium-sized, normal-shaped, dishwasher-safe wineglasses with stems. That's all you need. And with that, I'll stop and await my cease-and-desist letter from the Riedel company.

TOKAJI ASZÚ 5 PUTTONYOS

WHAT	Sweet white wine made mostly from the grape varieties Furmint and Hárslevelű
WHERE	Hungary
WHY	This nobly rotten nectar is exquisite sweet wine, delicious on its own and otherworldly with the right cheese.
PRONUNCIATION	*toh-kai-ee AH-soo five puh-TOHN-yosh*
HOW MUCH	Decent examples cost $40 to $60 (typically for 500 milliliters).
PAIR WITH	The strongest, funkiest cheese you can find

Tokaji Aszú 5 Puttonyos

Many countries take pride in their wines. Few take so much pride as to write wine into their national anthems. Here is the start of the third stanza of "Himnusz," the national anthem of Hungary: *Értünk Kunság mezein / Ért kalászt lengettél, / Tokaj szőlővesszein / Nektárt csepegtettél*. (For us on the plains of the Kunság / You ripened the wheat / In the grape fields of Tokaj / You dripped sweet nectar.) So yes, oftentimes when a Hungarian fencer earns an Olympic gold medal, he or she belts out a line about Tokaji's sweet nectar.

I understand the enthusiasm. Among the three prominent sweet wines affected by "noble rot" (Tokaji, Sauternes, Trockenbeerenauslese), Tokaji represents the most consistent value. That's not to say Tokaji is inexpensive. You'll need to spend at least $40 for a compelling bottle, and that bottle will only be two-thirds the size of a normal one. It's worth the splurge. You'd spend forty bucks easy for a few movie tickets and a bucket of popcorn; Tokaji will provide more visceral thrill than most cinematic experiences, and you can even pair it with popcorn if you like.

The reason Tokajis (and all the best sweet wines in the world) are expensive is that you're only paying for rich, unctuous nectar—not water. What most stickies have in common is that they come from extremely concentrated juice, and by that I mean juice with low water content. You can freeze that water content and press it out (ice wine/eiswein), or you can lay the grapes out on straw mats and let them raisin as the water content evaporates (Vin Santo).

Or, if you're lucky enough to live in a place where you get foggy mornings that encourage the growth of one particular type of fungus (*Botrytis cinerea*, also known as noble rot) but sunny afternoons to discourage other forms of mold and rot, and that place happens to also have a labor force that can make multiple trips through the vineyard, picking only the berries or clusters affected by the noble fungus, well then, you get to make the most thrilling sweet wines in the world.

The reason that *Botrytis*-affected stickies reign supreme is that they add as they take away. Freezing water, evaporating water—all that does is take away water. *Botrytis* does take away water (the fungus punctures small holes in grape skins, through which much of the grape's water content evaporates while the grape is still on the vine), but it also adds its own flavor. Identifying that exact flavor is tricky (honey, caramel, and mushroom pop up with some regularity; yellow curry even appears from time to time), so we turn to more general adjectives: earthy, lusty, carnal.

It's what makes Tokaji the main event of the night—a wine to contemplate over several hours. The best versions dazzle aromatically, with bittersweet marmalade, nut-studded toffee, minerality, and the kind of amatory kick that only a benevolent fungus can provide. Don't pair it with dessert; it's sweet enough to be dessert on its own. Instead, pair with a special piece of cheese or a special person (or both; I know I wouldn't like to be forced to choose).

May Meal

Shioyaki Salmon with Pea Salad

SALMON THIRTY SALMON

On the last day of March in 1987, a foot-long fish, one whose fate had heretofore seemed sealed, somehow escaped the clutches of an eagle's talons. I imagine the fish ever so briefly toasting his good luck, right before slamming into the cockpit window of an Alaska Airlines 737, just aloft from a Juneau runway. That this story actually happened—and caused an hour-long delay (bet the gate agents loved giving that explanation)—was muddied in a major way by the fact that all news reports on the incident were printed on the following day: April 1.

This was no April Fool's joke; just another chapter in the long-running story of Alaska Airlines and their home state's massive fishery. These days, the most prominent sign of that relationship is a 737-800 painted with a 129-foot Alaska king salmon. The plane is fondly known as the "salmon thirty salmon."

Each year, denizens of Seattle wait with bated breath for the arrival of the first salmon thirty salmon flight of the year. (Or, if not all denizens, at least ichthyophilic gastronome denizens with borderline obsessive-compulsive disorder.) That landing at Sea-Tac Airport, typically in mid-May, signifies the opening of months-long fresh salmon season, and the cargo hold contains tons of salmon pulled from the Copper River watershed, the first Alaskan river to see spring spawning.

Now perhaps this is the part where you think I'm going to delve into the long-running argument about the merits of Copper River salmon—is it PR hocus-pocus? or legitimate "merroir"?—and maybe I would be interested in the finer points of that particular debate if it hadn't been *seven entire months* since I last sank my teeth into a fresh piece of salmon.

A beautiful jewel of king or sockeye from the Copper River is never more expensive than it is in May, but this is one of those times when it's best to ignore restraint, patience, and good old common sense in favor of immediate gratification.

Shioyaki Salmon
with Pea Salad

Okay, so you just spent an unseemly portion of your last paycheck for a glistening hunk of sockeye salmon. Are you going to cook it using an avant-garde preparation and top it with a bold, aggressive sauce? No, you are not.

You're going to use a timeless Japanese preparation called *shioyaki* (salt-grilled) that is the height of simplicity. And you're going to top it with nothing. (I suppose a squeeze of lemon is acceptable. Marginally.)

Makes 4 servings

4 (6-ounce) sockeye salmon fillets	1 tablespoon canola oil, divided	1 medium lemon, cut into half-moons (optional)
2 teaspoons kosher salt	Pea Salad (recipe follows)	

Prepare the salmon. Sprinkle the fillets all over with kosher salt and then let them sit, uncovered, in the refrigerator for about 4 hours (really, anything from 2 to 24 hours will work just fine). This technique helps to deeply season the entire fish and encourages silky texture in the finished product.

Prepare the grill. Preheat a gas grill to 450 degrees F, or a charcoal grill with an entire chimney's worth of charcoal. Rub about a third of the canola oil on the grill grates.

Grill the salmon. Rub the salmon with the remaining canola oil. Lay the fillets on the grill, skin side up, and cook, uncovered, for 90 seconds. Using a large spatula, gently flip them over, cover the grill, and cook for another 4 to 7 minutes. (I like to start checking internal temperature after 3 minutes.) As soon as the fillets hit 125 degrees F, use a wide spatula to transfer them to a serving plate.

Serve. Plate each piece of salmon next to a scoop of pea salad, top with a slice of lemon, and encourage everyone to eat the salmon skin too, which should be grilled to salty-crispy-fishy perfection. ▶

Pea Salad

You're going to need something to distract you from staring at the salmon as it salt-cures. Shelling English peas should do the trick. This is the kind of pea whose pods are inedible to all nonruminants, but whose peas are large, luscious, and bursting with the green flavor of spring.

The linchpin of this salad is Taiwanese black vinegar, which is like a smokier, more floral, less sweet version of balsamic. Also, please note that Aunt Jemima is barely tolerable for pancakes and definitely not at all for salad dressings. Real maple syrup only, please.

Makes 4 servings

1 cup uncooked farro
¾ cup raw hazelnuts
½ cup extra-virgin olive oil
¼ cup Taiwanese black vinegar

2 tablespoons real maple syrup
½ teaspoon kosher salt
1 cup shelled English peas (from about ½ pound unshelled peas)

3 cups peavines (as small and tender as possible)

Cook the farro. In a medium saucepan over high heat, bring 3 cups of salted water to a boil. Add the farro, reduce the heat, cover, and simmer until tender, 40 to 60 minutes. Set aside to cool.

Toast the hazelnuts. Preheat the oven to 350 degrees F. Spread the hazelnuts in a single layer on a rimmed baking sheet, and toast until they just begin to brown, 10 to 15 minutes. Let cool, roughly chop, then set aside.

Prepare the dressing. In a medium bowl, whisk together the olive oil, vinegar, maple syrup, and salt. (Note: You will have more than enough dressing; any excess will keep in the refrigerator for about a month.)

Cook the peas. In a medium saucepan over high heat, bring 4 cups of salted water to a boil. Add the peas and boil until tender, 90 seconds to 3 minutes. Drain the peas and chill in a cold-water bath.

Assemble the salad. In a large bowl, combine the farro, drained peas, and peavines. Toss with enough dressing to wilt the vines. Just before serving, top with the hazelnuts.

Substitutions and Notes: Most Asian groceries will carry black vinegar, but if you can't source it, Sherry vinegar is an acceptable substitute. Peavines and English peas both have short seasons. If they're unavailable, spinach and snap peas, respectively, will both work fine.

Pairing: Pinot Noir is the classic salmon pairing, but with this meal, I'd reach for a Grüner Veltliner. In addition to having enough textural heft and bright acidity to complement the salmon, Grüner's savory lentil and sweet pea notes make it an exceptional pairing with the pea salad as well, the green notes in the food and the wine enhancing one another.

SAVOIE BLANC

WHAT	Dry white wine made from one of the grape varieties Jacquère, Altesse, or Bergeron (Roussanne)
WHERE	Eastern France, near the alpine border with Switzerland
WHY	Some of the best white wine values in the world come from Swiss ski country at the foot of the Alps.
PRONUNCIATION	*sah-VWA blohng*
HOW MUCH	Decent examples cost $10 to $20.
PAIR WITH	Cheese fondue, *queso fundido*, grilled ham and cheese; you get the picture

Savoie Blanc

Some of the finest white wine values in the world right now, dramatically underpriced for their inherent quality, come from ski-and-fondue country in eastern France, right up against the border with Switzerland. In the foothills of the Alps, growers and winemakers are producing pure, thrilling, crystalline wines, chock-full of alpine character. Most of the wines are gobbled up by the captive ski-resort audience, but in recent years, we've seen more and more Savoie whites hit our shores, and they're worth seeking out wherever you can find them.

We all gravitate toward the known, and that means we end up paying a familiarity tax. When we buy a bottle of Chardonnay, we're paying for the wine, and we're also paying a little upcharge because there's no sales effort required from a retailer or sommelier. The grape's reputation sells itself.

The inverse case: we have to be bribed to try unfamiliar varieties, and that bribery serves as a price-suppression mechanism. To wit: Jacquère and Altesse and Bergeron, the triumvirate of Savoie white varieties. Jacquère is the gateway into the world of Savoie whites, often hitting a $10 price point and offering a tasting experience that is less about overt fruit notes and more about minerals and lightly herbal notes. Imagine an alpine spring burbling over rocks and wildflowers and wild herbs: that's Jacquère.

More rare is Altesse (sometimes labeled *Roussette de Savoie*). Altesse possesses Jacquère's mountain-spring minerality and alpine fruit character, but it ratchets up the intensity, adds compelling dark floral tones (like violets), and has the acid backbone to age successfully for five to ten years, taking on nutty complexities with time in bottle. Finally there's Bergeron, the local name for Roussanne. This grape is best known in the Rhône Valley, where good versions of Rhône whites can run in the $50 to $100 range. Savoie Bergeron often comes in around twenty bucks and possesses several of the same qualities—haunting aromatics of peaches and raw almonds and chamomile tea, beautiful fruit density with no excess weight—all filtered through the minerality that seems to imprint itself on every Savoie white.

A popular pairing with Savoie whites in the ski lodges of the region is raclette, which refers to a type of cheese as well as a dish based on that cheese. The dish involves slowly melting the cheese and scraping it onto plates, alongside charcuterie, cornichons, and small boiled potatoes. What to drink with raclette has long been a subject of vigorous debate in the Savoie, to the point where a team of researchers actually published a 2010 study in the *British Medical Journal* titled "Effect on gastric function and symptoms of drinking wine, black tea, or schnapps with a Swiss cheese fondue: randomised controlled crossover trial." (Oh to be a participant in that one.) The study concluded that drinking wine "slowed gastric emptying," which is a good thing; no one wants to be the post-raclette gassy guest in the chalet bunkhouse.

Côte de Brouilly

A delicate, ethereal French red wine, expressive of the place it's grown, full of propulsive energy, with fruit that evokes the snap of biting into an ultra-fresh berry, and with an abiding sense of crushed-rock minerality. Yes, this describes good red Burgundy Pinot Noir that often requires a small mortgage to purchase. But it also describes some of the world's finest red wine values: Cru Beaujolais.

There's Beaujolais and then there's Beaujolais, and that has become a serious problem for serious winemakers in the region. The problem is that the Beaujolais most of us think of when we hear the term is Beaujolais Nouveau, an unabashed marketing success for the region. Harvested in August and September, Nouveau is fermented and bottled with lightning speed and released to the world on the third Thursday in November. The cash flow for wineries is nearly instantaneous, and the double edge of the sword is that we as consumers are price-anchored to think of Beaujolais as $10 wine.

CÔTE DE BROUILLY

WHAT	Dry red wine made from the grape variety Gamay Noir
WHERE	The slopes of Mont Brouilly, just north of the city of Lyon in France
WHY	This is radically different Beaujolais than the Nouveau you may be used to, and it's an outstanding value alternative to Pinot Noir.
PRONUNCIATION	*koht duh broo-yee*
HOW MUCH	Decent examples cost $15 to $25.
PAIR WITH	Coq au vin, especially if the *vin* in question is Côte de Brouilly

The other Beaujolais, Cru Beaujolais, comes from a series of ten tiny subregions, called *crus*. Often the wineries that produce Cru Beaujolais won't even print the word *Beaujolais* on their label (or it appears in microscopic font). Better to just emphasize their particular cru: Morgon, Fleurie, Moulin-à-Vent, or—my favorite—Côte de Brouilly. That way they can avoid the association with their cheap-and-cheerful ten-buck brethren and attempt to command higher prices.

It has been an uphill battle. While the best red Burgundies command thousands of dollars, the best Côte de Brouilly command . . . fifty bucks. Unfair, really, to the winemakers, but a complete windfall for those of us who love the wines.

I especially love the wines during the warmer months. While we often associate Beaujolais with Thanksgiving time (again, a vestige of Nouveau's third-Thursday release), Cru Beaujolais are pitch-perfect wines for early summer: light-bodied, ethereal, thirst-quenching. I'm especially fond of Côte de Brouilly because it is a tweener style of Gamay—not too light and not too serious—and because Côte de Brouilly is a small, special place—a region entirely circumscribed within the slopes of the extinct volcano Mont Brouilly. Those volcanic-soil slopes reach a grade of 50 percent, which in France is appropriate for two things: grape growing and bike racing. The top of Mont Brouilly often ends a stage in the famous Paris–Nice road cycling race, and it also contains the Notre-Dames-aux-Raisins (Our Lady of the Grapes) chapel, built in 1854 after a string of natural disasters (frost, hail, mildew) decimated three successive vintages on the mountain in the early 1850s. The inscription on the altar reads *À Marie contre l'oïdium*: "To Mary, against powdery mildew," which does lack a certain poetry you'd expect from a chapel inscription, but it gets points, as a memo to management, for clarity of message.

Serving Temperature

We all know that guy. The one who orders a glass of red wine out at a restaurant and then asks for some ice on the side. With devil-may-care insouciance, he drops a cube or two right into the center of his wine, and the ripples that reverberate around the glass are echoed by the whispers and titters that spread concentrically to surrounding tables. Well, I'm here to tell you: that fellow's means may be questionable, but his end is spot-on.

Serving temperature is an aspect of wine that we're all liable to get wrong. In short, we often drink our whites too cold and our reds too warm. A white wine directly out of a cold fridge will be 35 to 40 degrees F, cold enough to suppress just about every aromatic feature. It's no mistake that purveyors of cheap beer often encourage drinkers to chill their cans close to freezing. Temperatures that cold mask aromatic flaws, but with a nice white wine, that's precisely the opposite of what we want. Oftentimes you may notice that your white wines "open up" aromatically after a half hour or so. That has less to do with the wine's exposure to oxygen and more with the wine ascending to a temperature where aromatic compounds can be, well, aromatic.

Reds have the opposite problem. Anyone who recommends drinking red wine at "room temperature" should have their wine-advice license revoked. I suspect room temperature in Fairbanks in February will be different than mid-July Phoenix. The term is so vague as to be useless. And furthermore, just about every room temperature is too warm, with most reds served at temperatures that cause their alcohols to bloom more than is necessary. There's a special place in wine hell for restaurants that store their reds on high shelves in the hottest sections of their buildings.

Aim to serve whites at 45 to 50 degrees F, reds at 55 to 65 degrees F. Lighter whites and reds should be served at the lower ends of the spectrums, fuller whites and reds at the higher end. The half-hour rule of thumb works well for both categories. Pull whites from the fridge 30 minutes before serving. Put reds into the fridge for 30 minutes before serving. And save the ice cubes for negronis.

CAVA

WHAT	Dry sparkling wine made mostly from the grape varieties Macabeo, Parellada, and Xarel-lo
WHERE	The Penedès area of Catalonia, just outside of Barcelona in Spain
WHY	Cava offers the same production method used in Champagne but at cut-rate pricing.
PRONUNCIATION	*kah-vuh*
HOW MUCH	Decent examples cost $10 to $20.
PAIR WITH	Peach nectar for a perfect spring bellini

Cava

Let's just take it as a given that we should all be drinking more sparkling wine. I mean, seriously, how often are you disappointed when you open a bottle of bubbly? Approximately never percent of the time? I love sparkling wine during the first warm days of early summer. Maybe on its own, maybe as an aperitif with a dash of Aperol, maybe mixed into a bellini or a mimosa with the first brunch once it's warm enough to eat out on the deck or porch or lawn. This is the time of year when I look for sparkling wines that are reasonably priced, versatile, and—importantly—fairly neutral (characterful bubblies are squandered when mixed with assertive flavors like Aperol or peach nectar). In June I turn to Cava.

Cava and Prosecco are often lumped into the same basket: inexpensive European sparkling wine that isn't Champagne. But the two are actually quite different. Nearly all sparkling wines have to go through two fermentations: the first is when yeast turns grape sugar into alcohol (the "base wine") and the second when small amounts of additional yeast and sugar are added to create a bit more alcohol, along with the all-important carbon dioxide bubbles.

Prosecco performs its second fermentation in large pressurized tanks, while Cava does so in bottle. That puts Cava much closer to Champagne's production method than Prosecco's, and likely helps explain why Cava was called Champaña until 1970, at which point the brand-protective Champenois agitated successfully for a rename. While the recipe may be similar to Champagne, Cava's ingredients are totally different: different soils (none of the chalk that underlies Champagne) and very different grapes. While two of Champagne's three main varieties are red (Pinot Noir and Pinot Meunier, alongside Chardonnay), all three of Cava's main varieties are white, and chances are you've heard of none of them: Macabeo, Parellada, and Xarel-lo.

The yields in Cava are allowed to be higher than in Champagne, and the maturation time is allowed to be shorter, both of which allow for more delicate, austere, neutral sparkling wines, and both of which encourage lower price tags. That's not true, of course, for every Cava. There are some producers that mimic Champagne in low yields and long bottle-maturation times (and in prices), but those are the bottles for special occasions. For workhorse June bubbly, an honest, refreshing, $15 Cava is just the thing. Two wineries (Freixenet and Codorníu) represent a staggering 75 percent of all Cava production, but boutique beauties abound in the remaining 25 percent. Seek them out.

June Meal

Saffron-Butter Spot Prawns with a Simple Salad and Strawberries

TO MARKET

The rapid proliferation of farmers' markets is the greatest American food trend I can think of in my lifetime. In 1994, the United States Department of Agriculture counted 1,755 farmers' markets nationally. By 2016, the number was 8,669. That's a lot more radishes available to us plebs. (Not to mention overscented candles and shoddily thrown pottery).

I used to wonder sometimes when I would go out to a restaurant: Why is this food so much better than what I make at home? And okay, yes, I acknowledge that one factor was the whole years-of-professional-training thing, but still. Even the salads were better! And not because of some complicated dressing. The lettuces themselves were more characterful, with snap and crunch and personality. I quickly came to realize: restaurant food tasted better because good restaurants were starting with better building blocks. They had relationships with good farmers, farmers who grew crops with an eye toward flavor and quality, not toward supermarket priorities of size and veneer.

Gaining access to farmers' markets allows home cooks to close the gap a little on the restaurant pros. We still can't match their technique or the BTUs of their burners, but at least we can start from something approaching a level playing field.

Saffron-Butter
Spot Prawns

I'm lucky to live in Seattle, where a working farmers' market doubles as a massive tourist attraction. Realize that the guys who throw the fish are not just doing it for spectacle; they throw the fish that a customer has purchased and intends to take home and cook and eat.

Pike Place Market has a number of seafood vendors, and in May and June, they often carry fresh live spot prawns. These are Pacific shrimp that range from Alaska to Southern California. For decades, the vast majority were exported to Japan, where they are considered a sushi delicacy (*ama ebi*), but in recent years, West Coasters have begun to catch on to what the Japanese have known for years: these shrimp are exquisite. Their flavor is sweet and succulent, their texture delicate and springy. This is a far cry from bland-and-rubbery shrimp cocktail made from imported Southeast Asian shrimp.

While the season to buy spot prawns alive and fresh is short, they freeze well, which extends their season considerably and which also makes them available for air shipping (Pike Place Fish Market is a reliable vendor). This preparation assumes that you're starting with prawns whose heads have been removed, but if you're lucky enough to start with head-on prawns, be sure to suck all the juices out of those heads. Sounds gross, tastes great.

These delicate little sea creatures are easily overcooked, which will render them tough and rubbery. Err on the side of undercooking them, and note that in Japan they're just as happy eating them raw.

Makes 4 servings

1 cup (2 sticks) unsalted butter

3 cloves garlic, finely chopped

Zest and juice from 1 medium lemon

1 generous pinch saffron (about ¼ teaspoon)

1 baguette

2 pounds shell-on spot prawns

Finely chopped fresh parsley, for garnish

▶

Prepare the flavored butter. In a medium saucepan over medium heat, heat the butter until melted. Add the garlic and cook until fragrant, 1 to 2 minutes. Stir in the lemon zest and saffron and turn off the heat. The zest and saffron will steep in the warm butter while you cook the prawns.

Blanch the prawns. Preheat the oven to 350 degrees F. In a large (16-quart) stockpot over high heat, bring 8 quarts of salted water to a boil. (Alternatively, if you don't own a large stockpot, split the prawns into two batches with 4 quarts of salted water in each pot). While the water comes to a boil, throw the baguette into the oven to warm. Add the prawns to the pot and cook at a rolling boil until pink and tender: start checking at 30 seconds, but it should take no more than 2 minutes. Drain and transfer the prawns to a large serving bowl.

Serve. Drizzle the flavored butter and lemon juice over the prawns and toss until all are coated with a gold-orange saffron-butter sheen, then garnish with parsley. Bring the serving bowl and warm baguette to the table and let everyone eat with their hands, tearing pieces of baguette, pulling the shells off the prawns, and dipping into the leftover butter.

Simple Salad
with Honey–Fish Sauce Dressing

The first year I put in a raised-bed garden in our side yard, I made the rookie mistake of planting all our lettuce starts at the same time. I quickly went from optimism (aw, look at those cute little starts growing in our yard) to excitement (wow! those puppies are growing fast!) to horror (*how* are we going to eat this much lettuce?). Here's the dressing that emerged as the champion of our over-lettuced summer. The type of lettuce you drizzle it over doesn't really matter here; just grab the most beautiful, freshest-looking head you can find.

Makes 4 servings

1 tablespoon honey

¼ cup mayonnaise (preferably Hellmann's/ Best Foods)

¼ teaspoon fish sauce

1½ tablespoons brown rice vinegar

1 large head lettuce

Prepare the dressing. In a medium microwave-safe bowl, microwave the honey until melted, about 20 seconds (this will make it much easier to whisk into a dressing). Add the mayonnaise, fish sauce, and vinegar, whisking until smooth. (Note: You will have more than enough dressing; any excess will keep in the refrigerator for up to a month.)

Toss the salad. Tear the lettuce into bite-size pieces and place in a large serving bowl. Add the dressing one spoonful at a time and toss until the leaves are just barely—and evenly—coated (remember: we want to celebrate the lettuce, not mask it). Hands work better than utensils for gentle tossing.

Serve. I like to serve this salad after the spot prawns course. The combination of the fresh snap of the lettuce and the sour tang of the dressing helps to hit the palate reset button. It's a refreshing interlude before the closing act of fresh strawberries.

Strawberries

I still remember being struck, in early farmers' market visits, by how eager the vendors were for us to sample their products. And it didn't take long to understand why. The first time I bit into a local mid-June strawberry—a tiny, blood-red-to-its-core flavor grenade—my life changed. My entire mental model of *strawberry* was completely upended. Someone had upgraded my conception of strawberry from standard definition to high-def. There was no going back.

For strawberries like that, I suggest no preparation at all. If the berries are good enough, whipped cream, brown sugar, and the like just get in the way.

Enough for 4 servings
2 pints local strawberries

Serve. Place the unhulled berries in a large bowl at the center of the table, and remove all utensils. Revel in the childlike pleasure of picking each berry up by its stem and biting into a perfect, juicy morsel.

Substitutions and Notes: If you can't source spot prawns, we have another fine American fishery for shrimp in the Gulf of Mexico. Regular rice vinegar is a fine substitute for brown rice vinegar.

Pairing: While a Savoie white would be lovely with the prawns, if I'm considering the entirety of the meal, I'd reach for Cava, which pairs as effortlessly with vinaigrettes and berries as it does with seafood.

RÍAS BAIXAS ALBARIÑO

WHAT	Dry white wine made from the grape variety Albariño
WHERE	The Atlantic northwest of Spain
WHY	Albariño grown in this part of Spain mixes lemon-lime fruit with salty minerality to make a deeply refreshing summer white.
PRONUNCIATION	*REE-ahs BI-shess ahl-bah-REE-nyoh*
HOW MUCH	Decent examples cost $15 to $20.
PAIR WITH	Calamari, or roasted octopus, or really any cephalopod within grabbing distance

Rías Baixas Albariño

Albariño from Rías Baixas, given a hard chill on a hot day, is one of summer's great pleasures. It's Sprite for adults, with all the lemon-lime citric goodness we've come to expect, but with the added benefit of alcohol instead of straight sugar. Good Rías Baixas also has this subtle, but insistent, salty minerality that I don't remember from the "magic ice cubes" of my youth (frozen Sprite cubes, my mother's palliative for childhood sore throats).

When we think of Spain, we often think of its warm Mediterranean side—Barcelona, Valencia—or its scorching interior. But when it comes to wine, many of Spain's gems are unearthed by scouring Spain's deep-green, oft-forgotten Atlantic coast. This cool-climate area produces crisp, refreshing white wines that populate my fridge every single summer.

Galicia, in a rainy corner of Spain's Atlantic northwest, is culturally distinctive, including a long history of Celtic influence. To this day, residents play bagpipes and eat potatoes. Only instead of eating those potatoes alongside haggis, they eat them with octopus and hake and all manner of crustaceans that ply the cold waters just off the coast.

If the cuisine is idiosyncratic, so too is the wine, which centers on Albariño from Rías Baixas. The name of the region describes the four lower (*baixas*) river estuary inlets that dot the area. There is still some debate over whether Albariño is indigenous to the region or arrived via traveling monk from other parts of Europe, but it is clearly suited to this part of Spain. Albariño has thick skins, making it resistant to the rots and fungi that turn up in Galicia's humid climes, and it doesn't require much heat during the growing season to produce a white wine full of character and texture.

Albariño pairs beautifully with the cuisine of the region. And by that I mostly mean seafood (although I'm sure it's also lovely with potatoes). It has delicate enough flavors to pair with easily overwhelmed dishes like seared scallops (wines with more robust flavors only mask the scallops' sweet subtlety), and Albariño's grace note of salinity seems custom-tailored to drink alongside creatures pulled from the depths of briny waters, Spanish or closer to home.

California Zinfandel

Let me pause and underscore, before we get any further, that I'm talking about *red* Zinfandel—the one that makes robust red wines, filled with berry jam and brambles and savories like roasted rosemary and tomato paste, just right for the bold summer cookout flavors of ribs and pulled pork and smoked brisket. Not to be confused with White Zinfandel, the semisweet patio pounder that I'd like to make extensive fun of, except for the underlying hypocrisy of the fact that my first wine experience was Beringer White Zin from my parents' ice-cold basement fridge, and which launched mine and I'm certain many others' affections toward this beverage we hold dear.

If there is one grape variety that is a truly American story, it is Zinfandel. Yes, you wine-nerd pickers of nits, I will acknowledge that Zinfandel is a genetic match to southern Italy's Primitivo, and both are genetic matches to Crljenak Kaštelanski, which I know looks like my cat just walked across my keyboard but which is in actual fact a grape indigenous to Croatia. Still: Zinfandel ripens differently and expresses itself differently in California than anyplace else in the world, and it is tightly interwoven with our complicated boozy history.

The United States was only a half-century old when Zinfandel arrived on the East Coast and took the garden hothouses by storm. When California's gold rush hit in the late 1840s, it sent all manner of folks west, including nurserymen who brought their Zinfandel vines with them, and who found that the vines thrived outside of hothouses in California's favorable climate. With a near-to-unquenchable thirst for booze among the burgeoning miner class, vineyards were planted widely in the 1850s and 1860s.

Remarkably, some of those vines are still in production today. There's documentary evidence of one Zinfandel vineyard, planted in 1869, that still produces usable grapes as it closes in on its 150th birthday. Vineyards like this even survived Prohibition, mostly on the backs of home winemakers (each household could annually produce two hundred gallons of wine—or other fermented juice—for on-site consumption).

CALIFORNIA ZINFANDEL

WHAT	Dry red wine made from the grape variety Zinfandel
WHERE	California in the United States, preferably from Sonoma County or one of its sub-appellations
WHY	Zinfandel is a truly American red wine, historically intertwined with our past. Its bold flavors and robust texture make it brilliant with the food of summer cookouts and barbecues.
PRONUNCIATION	*ZIN-fen-dell*
HOW MUCH	Decent examples cost $15 to $40.
PAIR WITH	One of those barbecue plates that includes the pulled pork *and* the brisket *and* the smoked sausages

Wine Packaging

I'm an enthusiastic proponent of alternative wine packaging. Glass bottles represent about 85 percent of all wine packaging, but I'd be surprised if they're necessary in more than about 10 percent of wines. If you're buying expensive wine, meant to age for years in a temperature-controlled cellar, yes, you should seek out cork-finished glass bottles of wine. You should also keep a pristine cloth on hand for cleaning your monocle.

For the rest of us, the outside packaging is much less important than the juice inside, and it quickly becomes difficult to justify the weight and cost and environmental impact of heavy glass. Here are some alternative packages on the rise:

Bag-in-box wines usually come in three-liter boxes (the equivalent of four bottles of wine), while *Tetra Paks* are often the same size as a glass bottle (750 milliliters) or a little bigger (1 liter). They're wonderful for outdoor activities like picnics (they hold their temperature well, so whites and Rosés stay nice and cold) and camping trips (they're considerably lighter than glass), and they'll remain fresh for weeks in the fridge. There's still a cheap/bad wine stigma attached to this packaging, but it's dissipating quickly. It reminds me of how we viewed screw-cap bottles ten years ago, and I suspect in another decade we'll see these boxes as perfectly acceptable packaging for quality wines.

Cans serve the needs of those of us who want a single drink (or maybe two if it's been that kind of day). Most cans range from 187 milliliters (a quarter bottle) to 375 milliliters (a half bottle). Again, they're lighter and more portable than glass, this time so portable, in fact, that they can fit into a coat pocket and be snuck into a movie theater to pair with good popcorn and bad dialogue.

Single-serve cups are without question the silliest emerging alternative packaging. They're often sold in connected stacks of four that look like sex toys for a race of giants. You split the stack, pull back the foil on top, and you've got drink and vessel, all in one. I get the convenience factor, but having all those cups is wasteful, and there's something infantilizing about how much these resemble the single-serve applesauce containers I put in my kids' lunches.

Zinfandel has such a deep shared history with California that one state senator, Carole Migden, authored a 2006 bill (SB 1253) designating Zinfandel as "California's historic wine." The bill actually passed both houses of California's legislature, only to meet then-governor Arnold Schwarzenegger's veto hammer. He claimed that "singling one [variety] out for special recognition would be inappropriate." Senator Migden's disappointment was apparently leavened by her abiding love of puns: "While we were crushed by the veto," she said, "the governor will find no sour grapes in our office. Next year we will press on." Migden's reelection bid in 2008 was not successful.

Côtes de Provence Rosé

While we've been patiently glugging down bottles of last year's Rosé (see page 23) and domestic Rosé (see page 37), winemakers in the south of France have been bottling, consolidating, and shipping their own beautiful bottles of pink. Now, in July, container ships groaning under the weight of pallet after pallet of Provençal Rosé are arriving at ports up and down both coasts, ready to release a pink torrent onto a populace that just can't seem to get enough.

Rosé from Provence has been on a multiyear major upward trend in American consumption. In 2010, we drank something like one million liters of the stuff. By 2015, the number was eight million liters and growing. Along the way, pervasive old beliefs about Americans and Rosé—that we wouldn't drink bone-dry Rosé, that American men wouldn't drink Rosé, period—were exposed as inane retrograde bullshit.

Good for us for recognizing quality and embracing it! While our domestic Rosé trade has made major strides in recent years, Provence is unquestionably the beating heart of Rosé production in the world. The best versions are made from thin-skinned Grenache and Cinsault, perfectly suited to impart a pale-pink hue to each Rosé they touch. Flavors combine

CÔTES DE PROVENCE ROSÉ

WHAT	Dry Rosé made most commonly from the grape varieties Grenache, Cinsault, Mourvèdre, and Carignan
WHERE	Provence, in the south of France
WHY	Provence is the world's capital of dry, crisp Rosé production, and these wines are wonderfully refreshing in midsummer.
PRONUNCIATION	*koht duh pro-VAWNSS ro-ZAY*
HOW MUCH	Decent examples cost $10 to $20.
PAIR WITH	Bouillabaisse or any other rustic fish stew

fruit notes (berry and melon and citrus) with minerality and a refreshing verdant edge, something like green strawberries muddled with chopped cucumbers. The wines are low in alcohol and high in mouthwatering acidity. On a hot July day, that first sip of cold Provençal Rosé is as bracing as a cold gust from the famous mistral winds that scour Provence's vineyards with alpine air.

We Yanks are not the first to be attracted to this sun-soaked Mediterranean corner of France. The Romans made it their first province outside the confines of Italy, calling it *provincial nostra* ("our province"). You can almost forgive the lack of naming creativity (akin to the Brits calling the United States "our colony") because of the clear affection reflected in the name. This beautiful blessed place, this is our province; keep your grubby mitts off it. By the time the Romans arrived (around 125 BC), the region already had a four-centuries-old winemaking tradition courtesy of the Greeks who predated them, and who seemed to have an uncanny ability to spot the right vineyard sites in every clime, like veteran teachers picking out the most promising students on day one of class.

The Greeks founded present-day Marseille (then called Massalia), and that city remains the heart of gustatory Provence. The most famous dish of the region—bouillabaisse—is a fish stew that seems like it was developed specifically with Rosé pairing in mind. Those bony, funky little Mediterranean fish overpower many a white wine and taste dissonant next to most reds; Rosé is the Goldilocks. If you can't slurp bouillabaisse and Rosé at a quayside Marseille bistro, if all the responsibilities of adult life—jobs, kids, neurotic cats—make a trip like this impossible, fear not: the container ship that began its journey alongside that Marseille quay is heading west, at speed.

Red-Blooded American Cheeseburger with Grilled Corn

THE ALTAR OF BURGER SIMPLICITY

There are times of the year when I'm okay with a baroque burger. You know what I mean, right: burgers with a twist? Like cheese inside the patty instead of atop it (the ol' Jucy Lucy [sic]). Or elaborate seasonings (*piment d'Espelette*, shallot powder). Or—*gasp*—a burger made from something other than beef.

We've all had our flings with jalapeño turkey burgers and seitan kimchi burgers and teriyaki ostrich burgers. There's no shame in playing the field. But when July hits and you're standing outside in the fresh air, photosynthesizing sunshine into endorphins while you wait for your charcoal to glow, it's time to set aside those one-night stands and return to old reliable. If we live in a time where it's hard to feel shamelessly patriotic about much, at least we have grass-fed, well-seasoned, red-blooded, perfectly grilled American cheeseburgers.

We're looking for the same characteristics in a burger that we look for in a good wine: intense flavor, perfect texture. There are many and varied ways to get it wrong, to fussify a good burger. Not today. Today we worship at the altar of burger simplicity, and we'll get there with the holy trinity of burger rules.

One: Start with good beef. I'm not one who believes you need to purchase chuck and grind it at home. If you have a good butcher, or a good grocery store butcher department, trust their grinding expertise. I *have* come to believe in the superiority of grass-fed beef. If you can source it, pay the few extra bucks per pound. I find that grass changes flavor intensity more than flavor character. A grass-fed burger still tastes like a burger, but more so; like replacing a light bulb with a higher-wattage version.

Two: Salt at the right time. Don't mix salt into the burger meat. When you do that, you're not making a burger, you're making sausage. The salt breaks down the beefy proteins, and you immediately eliminate any chance of the crumbly texture that makes a good burger toothsomely satisfying. Likewise, do not salt the patties immediately after forming them. You'll draw moisture to the surface of the patty, and when the burger hits the grill, you'll have created a steamer in miniature. Any chance of a crisp crust: up in smoke. The right time to salt the burger is immediately before it hits the grill, and then only the side of the patty that will be face down. Salt the other side just before flipping.

Three: Don't overcook. (And yeah, don't undercook either, but overcooking is the unrecoverable sin.) You can spend multiple summers learning the ins and outs of your particular grill and what exact amount of time a burger needs on each side to land on a crisp beefy crust and a perfectly medium interior. Or, if you don't have the patience for the "error" portion of trial and error, an instant-read thermometer will help enormously. Yes, you'll look like a schmohawk with your purple Thermapen in hand at the grill station, but your friends will forgive you when impeccably cooked burgers hit their plates.

Red-Blooded American Cheeseburger
with Grilled Corn

Following the rule trinity (see pages 100–101) is going to yield a groan-inducing burger. Your job now is to stay out of its way. Cheese should be subtle: American if it's actually the Fourth of July. Jack or (not-too-sharp) cheddar also works well. If you find yourself reaching for blue cheese or goat cheese or fontina, remind yourself that there are eleven other months of the year where robustly flavored cheeses on your burger are just fine. Likewise, use a simple grilled bun; this is not the time for ancient grains. Lay down a slice of perfectly ripe tomato for some acid to balance the richness of the burger. Maybe some butter on the buns or a squeeze of mayo if you really want to gild the lily.

I prefer to grill burgers with the lid closed. It speeds up the process, which keeps the outer edges of the burgers from drying out too much. As the folks at Weber Grills like to say: "If you're lookin', you ain't cookin'." Words to live by.

Makes 4 servings

1½ pounds grass-fed ground beef, formed into 4 patties
Kosher salt

4 slices jack, cheddar, or American cheese
4 hamburger buns
1 ripe tomato, thickly sliced

Grilled Corn with Pasture Butter and Smoked Salt (recipe follows)

Preheat the grill. Set a gas grill to high heat or prepare a full chimney's worth of charcoal for a charcoal grill.

Form the patties. The burgers will shrink a little as they cook, so make the patty diameters about ¼ inch larger than the buns. ▶

Grill the burgers. Season one side of each patty generously with salt and then immediately place that side down on the grill. Cover (with vents open) and grill for about 3 minutes. Just before flipping, season the top of each patty with salt. Flip and immediately lay a slice of cheese on each patty. Cover again and cook for about 3 more minutes, or until the internal temperature registers 130 degrees F. Transfer the burgers to a plate and allow them to rest for at least 5 minutes. This will bring the temperature up to 135 degrees F, on the rare side of medium.

Grill the buns. While the burgers are resting, add the buns to the grill, cover, and toast for a minute or two until browned and warmed through.

Serve. Place each burger on a bun. Add a slice of tomato. Add any other toppings you feel are necessary. (They're not.) Serve with the grilled corn.

Grilled Corn with Pasture Butter and Smoked Salt

This is the time of year when sweet corn drops to a dollar per ear or less. It's the perfect accompaniment to burgers, especially because it allows us to do all our cooking outdoors. Firing up an oven or a stovetop in an already-hot July kitchen is good as a climate-change sneak preview, and not much else.

I love smoked sea salt on corn, especially grilled corn. It picks up the mantle of smokiness from the corn's char and carries it across the entire palate.

Over the past few years, some grocery stores have started carrying a product called pasture butter. This deep-golden flavor bomb comes entirely from cows put out to fresh pasture over the summer (May through September), and the result is a butter bursting with grassy complexity. No one is going to complain if you schmear their corn with run-of-the-mill high-quality butter. But if you can find pasture butter, you can present corn on the cob that sings "Summertime" (Gershwin, Fresh Prince, and Sublime versions all acceptable).

Makes 4 servings

4 ears corn, shucked   Pasture butter,   Smoked sea salt,
                                   for serving   for serving

Grill the corn. Place the corn on the still-hot grill and cook, turning every few minutes, until tender and deeply charred, 10 to 15 minutes total.

Serve. Remove the corn from the grill and let your guests add butter and salt to taste. Keep wet wipes handy. ▶

Substitutions and Notes: The availability of pasture butter is still pretty iffy. If you can't find it, look for a European or European-style butter, which basically just means higher butterfat content. Any unsalted butter will work in a pinch. Likewise, kosher salt will be just fine if smoked salt is unavailable.

Pairing: A crisp pilsner would be just the thing on a hot summer's—oh wait, wrong book. While I would not fault anyone for making the classic burger-and-beer pairing, there are several wines that are outstanding with a good cheeseburger. This month, let's pair like with like, and eat this meal with a ripe, jammy California Zinfandel. This hedonist's delight should be served with a sidecar of Lipitor and a long nap in a hammock.

MUSCADET

WHAT	Dry white wine made from the grape variety Melon de Bourgogne
WHERE	In France, near the mouth of the Loire River as it flows into the Atlantic Ocean
WHY	This delicate, minerally, austerely fruited white is as brilliant with seafood (especially raw oysters) as it is on its own as a refreshing summer cocktail.
PRONUNCIATION	*MUSS-ka-day*
HOW MUCH	Decent examples cost $10 to $20.
PAIR WITH	Mussels steamed in wine, fish stock, lemon juice, and a splash of cream

Muscadet

Muscadet is a wine that charms with its subtlety. What little fruit shows up is simple citrus or green apple. But this is an austere, delicate wine by nature, much more about minerality and nervy acidity than overt fruit. Muscadet makes a lovely hot-weather aperitif—ice-cold, low-alcohol, and insistently neutral, which I'll admit does sound eerily similar to the selling points of Bud Light—but is unquestionably at its best when paired with seafood, especially shellfish. Each enhances the salty brininess of the other.

Modern Muscadet is the result of two happy accidents. The first happened when the area near the mouth of the Loire River was planted out broadly to the Melon de Bourgogne grape in the eighteenth century. It was planted at the urging of Dutch traders, who were looking for a white wine that was as high yielding and neutral as possible. Not for drinking. For distillation into high-octane spirits. And then for drinking. Because if you've just worked a long, arduous day in the chill of an Amsterdam November, do you want a delicate white wine? No, you want a trachea-melting brandy. As it turned out, the Muscadet that didn't end up on Dutch schooners and in Dutch copper stills paired perfectly with the cuisine of this part of France, heavily influenced by the nearby crustacean bounty of the Atlantic Ocean. Happy accident number one.

Happy accident number two took place when Muscadet producers began leaving some of their best barrels of wine undisturbed over the entire winter following harvest. Local lore took to calling these the "honeymoon barrels," likely because they helped consummate many a spring and summer marriage. Over time, winemakers noticed that their Muscadets' extra time in contact with dead yeast cells (a by-product of fermentation called *lees*) had a beneficial effect on the texture of the wine, plumping up and softening what are otherwise enamel-stripping acid bombs. Most imported Muscadet will include the term *sur lie* on the label, which means the wine was aged on its lees until bottling. And also means your teeth will be safe.

Chinon Rouge

"Twice or thrice praise Chinon town; / Little city: great renown. / Sited on an ancient Hoe, / Woods above, the Vienne below." That is the French humorist-gourmand (and Chinon native) François Rabelais, writing in his great work *Gargantua and Pantagruel*. Rabelais was a wine savant, intuiting aspects of wine appreciation that Master Sommelier classes still discuss. "Drink once, drink twice, drink thrice," a Rabelaisian character notes, "having a different wine in mind each time, and you will find the taste, the bouquet, and the feel on your tongue of whatever wine you thought of." That is the mental suggestibility of blind wine tasting, in nutshell form.

Much of the praise Rabelais lavishes upon Chinon is reserved for his hometown's vineyards, and seven centuries or so later, I heartily concur. Cabernet Franc from Chinon is among the most charming of red wines, and is certainly the greenest. Arugula, peppery watercress, braising greens: all turn up from time to time in Chinon tasting notes. These green savories often complement bright berry fruit and violet notes. The combination is unique, compelling, and just right for this time of year.

August is summer's twilight, autumn on the tips of our tongues. These are the last hot days of the year, and they bring a vegetable bounty at gardens and farmers' markets alike: tomatoes and cucumbers, zucchini and eggplant, peppers and beans. Most red wines overwhelm the flavors of these summer veggies, or they're simply too rich and alcoholic for a hot late-summer's day. Chinon, on the other hand, is light and refreshing and vegetal in the best possible way. Grown in the cool valley of the Loire River in France, Cabernet Franc rarely exceeds 13 percent alcohol.

That's a good thing. In warmer regions, where Franc is allowed to get riper, its profile converges with that of its genetic offspring, Cabernet Sauvignon (a cross of Cabernet Franc and Sauvignon Blanc). Ripe Cabernet Franc drinks like ripe Cabernet Sauvignon, offering rich berry and cassis fruit along with robust tannins. Nothing wrong with that, but it's indistinctive. Cool pockets like Chinon, on the other hand, allow Cabernet Franc to embrace its individuality, its inherent green-and-leafy nature.

CHINON ROUGE

WHAT	Dry red wine made from the grape variety Cabernet Franc
WHERE	The central Loire Valley in France
WHY	This region allows Cabernet Franc to express its inherently green nature, chock-full of vegetal notes (arugula, watercress) to complement its berry fruit.
PRONUNCIATION	*SHEE-nohn roozh*
HOW MUCH	Decent examples cost $15 to $30.
PAIR WITH	A ratatouille made from late-summer veggies at their peak

GETARIAKO TXAKOLINA

WHAT	Dry, semisparkling white wine made from the grape variety Hondarribi Zuria
WHERE	The village of Getaria in Spain's Basque Country, within view of the Atlantic Ocean's Bay of Biscay
WHY	This semisparkling wine—full of salt air and minerality—is served at every *pintxo* joint in San Sebastián. They're onto something.
PRONUNCIATION	*geh-TAH-ree-ah-ko chah-ko-LEE-nah*
HOW MUCH	Decent examples cost $10 to $20.
PAIR WITH	Fried mozzarella sticks or really anything emerging from a proper deep fryer

Getariako Txakolina

Walk into any *pintxo* (the Basque word for tapas) restaurant in San Sebastián, and before you remove your jacket and find a seat, you're likely to see the bartender grab a wine bottle, hold it well over his head, and pour from great heights into a large, flat-bottomed glass closer in looks to a pint glass than a traditional wineglass. The wine explodes into the glass and effervesces into a riot of tiny bubbles. Party started.

Txakolina's cleansing spritz is perfectly paired to the delirious absurdity of a full *pintxo* spread, with its oil-packed fishes and blood sausages, its *croquetas de jamón* and hard cheeses. The grapes come from vineyards thirty minutes west of San Sebastián, deep into Basque country. Vineyards are planted in the rolling hills above the seaside town of Getaria, the indigenous Hondarribi Zuria vines trained so high that a grown adult can walk beneath them.

The viticulture of the area and the local cuisine have grown up together and dovetail perfectly. Txakolina is harvested early to maintain its piercing natural acidity, and it is bottled under pressure to capture some of the residual carbon dioxide from fermentation (hence the cleansing sense of effervescence), all of that making it the perfect pairing for the grilled and fried seafood adored by denizens of a stretch of Atlantic coast running from San Sebastián to Bilbao. Walk back down the hills into Getaria in the golden light of late afternoon, and you'll see the ocean glimmering below, smell the wood smoke of a dozen outdoor grills firing up, and hear the pops of Txakolina bottles.

What little Txakolina escapes the clutches of Basque country is mostly destined for the trendy wine bars of Barcelona and Madrid. Only a tiny amount is imported into the United States, but it is well worth seeking out. In a future world of my making, Txakolina would be poured at state fairs all across America (into red Solo cups, naturally), the perfect wine for our national love affair with the deep fryer.

August Meal

Oysters Three Ways

SPARE-TIME OYSTER HARVESTER

In my spare time, I am an oyster harvester. Okay, wait. I probably ought to stop right there. That sentence evokes unwieldy diving gear. Appetite for danger. Macho disregard for hypothermia in the pursuit of tastier bivalves. Whereas the actual list of skills needed to harvest oysters is threefold: First, the ability to walk. Second, the ability to count. And third, the ability to discern the bigger of two objects. It does not escape me that all three are skills my toddlers picked up by the ripe old age of twenty-one months.

From Cape Cod to Puget Sound, a small but growing number of organizations offer something called Community Supported Aquaculture, which sounds like Soviet-style collectivist farming underwater but is actually a program whereby I (and many others) pay a sum early in the year for the right to a series of subsequent oyster harvests, as well as the right to feel like we're doing our part to improve local water quality. My family always opts for the largest possible membership: seventy-two oysters per month.

Now a skeptic might be asking: What does my family slurping over three hundred oysters each year have to do with improving water quality? Well, oysters are like miniature environmental remediators. They're filter feeders, and a healthy adult churns through more than a gallon of seawater per hour. The actual mechanism could be described as unappetizing—an oyster traps algae/plankton/sediment in its gill mucus before digesting those materials and expelling them as . . . wait for it . . . harmless oyster feces—but the end result does wonders for aquatic ecosystems. And happens to be delicious. (Despite the whole mucus-and-feces thing.)

The sluggard option for each monthly harvest is to simply pick your bagged oysters up at a designated oyster muster station, but the more vigorous option, the one I choose whenever possible, is to participate in the harvest. The oysters grow in mesh bags tied to a line that remains underwater during all but the lowest tides of each month. On an extra-low tide day, we intrepid harvesters scuttle down to the exposed bags, cut them off their lines, dump the bags onto blue tarps, and begin the "harvest."

Here is the entire process. Step 1: Sort each oyster by size as either keeper or put-back. Step 2: Separate the keepers into piles of a dozen oysters each. Step 3: Place those piles into member bags. As you might imagine, this process leaves ample time and brainpower for conversation among the harvest team. (Sample: "Don't you think a blue heron kind of looks like a pterodactyl?" "Kind of.") It also leaves time for "product testing," and I've learned over the years that a wise harvester will stash in his or her waterproof bib pants one shucking knife (required), one lemon (optional but recommended), and one 375-milliliter split of white wine (optional but strongly recommended).

Standing on a beach, shucking and eating an oyster that was underwater only minutes ago, talking story: it's a spiritually transcendent experience, offering common cause with thousands of years of oyster lovers who have been similarly graced by the aquatic abundance of the local waters.

Raw Oysters

I prefer smaller oysters for raw slurping, but (much) more important than the size or type of oyster is its freshness. The ideal is to find oysters harvested within the past twenty-four hours.

If you want to gussy up your oysters with hot sauce or olive oil or a fancy mignonette, well, I suppose that's your business, but I can't recommend it. In my oyster religion, if you're adding anything more than a few drops of freshly squeezed lemon juice, you're blaspheming.

Makes 6 servings

2 dozen fresh oysters, chilled

1 medium lemon, cut into half-moons (optional)

Serve. Shuck an oyster. Squeeze a few drops of lemon juice onto said oyster, if desired. Slurp. Repeat.

Panko-Fried Oysters

I've converted many an "I don't like oysters"-spouting bivalve-phobe to the naughty-wonderful world of oysters via this gateway-drug preparation, which uses layers of cornmeal and panko for added crunch factor. Crispy exterior. Creamy, briny center. Spicy dipping sauce. Game over. Next thing you know, they're slurping raw oysters right off the beach and wondering how they ever got by without these delicious mollusks.

Unless you want to spend all your time racing back and forth between the sink and the frying pan, enlist a helper for this one. With one person breading and one person frying, a sense of calm may just descend on the kitchen. That is, until the fried oysters are dropped onto a paper towel–covered plate, after which happy chaos will reign.

Makes 6 servings

½ cup mayonnaise (preferably Kewpie)
1 tablespoon soy sauce
1 teaspoon rice vinegar
Chili oil, for added heat (optional)
Peanut oil, for frying

1 cup all-purpose flour
2 tablespoons coarsely ground cornmeal
2 large eggs, beaten
1 cup panko bread crumbs

2 dozen fresh oysters, shucked
Kosher salt
1 medium lemon, cut into half-moons

Prepare the dipping sauce. In a medium bowl, mix the mayonnaise with the soy sauce and vinegar. Add chili oil a few drops at a time until the sauce reaches the desired spiciness level.

Heat the oil. When you are ready to move forward with cooking the oysters, prepare the pan for frying. Fill a large skillet with peanut oil to a depth of about ½ inch and place over medium-high heat until shimmering. Line a large plate with paper towels and set aside.

Bread the oysters. Whisk together the flour and cornmeal on one plate, and arrange it next to a bowl with the eggs and a plate of panko. Dredge each oyster first in the flour, then dip in the egg, and finally coat in panko. The sooner these hit the hot oil after coating, the better. Very quickly, your fingers will resemble miniature dough monsters. Power through it.

Fry the oysters. Drop the breaded oysters into the hot oil and fry until golden-brown, 2 to 3 minutes. Flip the oysters and fry for another 1 to 2 minutes. Remove to the paper towel–lined plate.

Serve. Many oysters are naturally salty enough that no additional seasoning is required, but taste one to be sure; if it's dull, drop a pinch of salt onto the remaining oysters after frying. Purists can throw these back with just a little squeeze of lemon, modernists with a generous dunk into the dipping sauce.

Oysters Rockefeller

Some combination of this dish's name and its price on restaurant menus always led me to think of it as a luxury item, appropriate for Rockefellers and their 1-percent kin. Then I started making it at home and realized that it's a humble, rustic dish, with mostly inexpensive ingredients. Out to dinner, Oysters Rockefeller feels like an indulgence. Made at home, it feels like good common sense.

The most important step in this recipe is pouring an even layer of rock salt (sometimes called ice cream salt) on a rimmed baking sheet. Nestled gently into these large salt cubes, the oysters will stay perfectly balanced, keeping all their briny-good liquor in the shell. That liquid gently steams the oyster from below, and condenses back into the shell alongside drops of good pastis. After eating each oyster, you'll be left with a thimbleful of warm anise-flavored liquor to slurp, a last reward for all your hard work.

Makes 6 servings

½ cup (1 stick) unsalted butter, divided

¼ cup minced fennel bulb

6 cloves garlic, minced

4 cups roughly chopped baby spinach

Kosher salt

1 cup pastis (such as Ricard)

1 cup panko bread crumbs

½ cup grated Parmesan cheese

2 cups rock salt

2 dozen fresh oysters

1 medium lemon, cut into half-moons

Prepare the spinach. Preheat the oven to 450 degrees F. In a large skillet over medium-high heat, melt 4 tablespoons of the butter. Add the fennel and garlic and sauté until just beginning to brown, 2 to 3 minutes. Add the spinach and a pinch of salt, cooking until the spinach wilts, another 2 to 3 minutes. Increase the heat to high, add the pastis, and boil until the liquid is reduced by about 90 percent, 5 to 10 minutes. Remove the pan from the heat and allow the mixture to cool to room temperature. ▶

Prepare the topping. In a medium microwave-safe bowl, melt the remaining 4 tablespoons butter. Stir in the panko and set aside to cool. Stir in the Parmesan cheese until evenly distributed.

Prepare the oysters. Pour the rock salt onto a rimmed baking sheet in an even layer. Shuck the oysters in their shells and nestle gently into the salt, spilling as little liquor as your dexterity and grace allow.

Assemble the Rockefellers. Spoon 1 tablespoon of the spinach mixture and 1 tablespoon of the topping onto each oyster. Bake for 15 to 20 minutes, or until the bread crumbs turn a deep golden-brown.

Serve. Eat the oysters piping hot, with a squeeze of lemon, using a fork to grab each one and then slurping whatever anise-and-lemon-tinged liquor remains.

Substitutions and Notes: Regular bread crumbs are fine for both the fried and Rockefeller oysters if panko is not available. Fennel bulb adds another layer of anise to the Oysters Rockefeller, but if you can't find it, there's really not a capable substitute; simply omit. If pastis is not available, any anise-flavored liquor will work: aquavit, absinthe, ouzo, sambuca.

Pairing: Drink delicate Muscadet with the raw oysters, and let fizzy Txakolina cut through the fried version. For the Rockefellers, serve Chinon Rouge. It will complement the spinach in the dish and emphasize the attractive earthiness of the oysters.

Wine Headaches

Okay, real talk. My chosen field is, alas, enduringly prone to bullshit. And we have no shortage of charlatans willing to capitalize on said bullshit to make a buck or two. An entire subcategory of wine, the no- and low-sulfide movement, is predicated on a group of people a) believing they're allergic to sulfides, and b) believing their sulfide allergy causes headaches. This is the gluten-free movement of the wine trade. As it happens, only about 1 percent of the population has a legitimate sulfur allergy, and, oops, that allergy doesn't cause headaches (it causes asthma symptoms, which I'm sure aren't fun either).

But okay, I'm willing to accept that some of you have experienced wine-related headaches with some regularity, and that you've talked to your therapists and confirmed that those headaches are not psychosomatic. For this group, let's say there are one hundred of you. One of you has a problem with amines, which are chemical compounds that are by-products of fermentation. Your test: eat an aged-cheese and charcuterie platter for dinner. And don't drink any wine! (I know those are good wine foods; sorry.) Those foods are also high in amines. Do you have a headache right now? No? Okay, it's not amines.

Another one of you might have a problem with tannins. These occur naturally in the skins and seeds of grapes, and they're considerably more prevalent in red wines than in whites. You know what else contains a boatload of tannins? Black tea. So go brew yourself a cup, drink it down, and report back. Still no headache? We've eliminated another culprit.

The remaining ninety-eight of you are suffering from headaches via what is, I'm afraid, a pedestrian reason, and yet—good news!—one that is easily fixed: you're dehydrated. Drinking wine—drinking any alcohol for that matter—has a dehydrating effect on the body. Your body pulls water from anyplace it can find, and that includes your brain. Commence headache. Fortunately, science has discovered a way to combat dehydration, and it is the consumption of water. Would you like a prescription from someone whose closest brush with medical school was living with a college roommate who was premed? Drink one glass of water for each glass of wine, and maintain a healthy skepticism about everything wine-related that you hear. (Unless I'm saying it, in which case it is of course bulletproof.)

SANTORINI ASSYRTIKO

WHAT	Dry white wine made from the grape variety Assyrtiko
WHERE	The Greek island of Santorini
WHY	Assyrtiko is the rare white wine that possesses both bright acidity and supple texture, making it perfect for a transition month like September.
PRONUNCIATION	*san-toh-REE-nee ah-SEER-tee-koh*
HOW MUCH	Decent examples cost $15 to $25.
PAIR WITH	Seafood risotto

Santorini Assyrtiko

On a small island in the middle of the Aegean Sea, thousands of what appear to be birds' nests are burrowed into a volcanic moonscape. From afar, it looks like an Andy Goldsworthy land art installation writ large. Wander closer during the long Greek summer, and you'll see life springing from these baskets. But not birds; instead the baskets are filled with green tendrils and leaves, and delicate bunches of grapes protected just beneath ground level. The island is Santorini, the grapes are Assyrtiko, and the resulting wines are among the most distinctive whites in the world.

The entire long winemaking history of this place is tied up in the volcano that produced the soil coating Santorini's hillside vineyards. Sometime around 1600 BC, one of the largest volcanic eruptions in human history turned much of the island of Thera into a collapsed-caldera underwater graveyard. What remained aboveground, including the Minoan settlement of Akrotiri, was buried in a layer of lava and ash so thick that the region was rendered uninhabitable for more than two hundred years. As archaeologists excavated the ruins of Akrotiri, they found that some of the charcoal originated as vine wood, evidence of a winemaking tradition dating back more than three millennia.

Modern winemaking on Santorini has faced its own challenges (fortunately an erupting volcano not among them), mostly centered on the winds that whip ceaselessly up off the Aegean. These winds scatter everything left aboveground: flowers and buds and grape berries alike. The only solution: take the grape-growing underground. Farmers on the island have devised an ingenious vine-training regimen, where they cudgel the vine into the shape of a small basket. This basket, called a *kouloura*, serves as a windbreak, a protector for the delicate grapes inside.

Mechanical harvesting is impossible under these conditions. Every cluster must be picked individually, on hands and knees. The labor would hardly seem worth it unless the resulting wines were special. Assyrtiko, an indigenous variety that comprises three-quarters of the island's plantings, is special indeed.

To begin with, Assyrtiko grapes retain an unusual amount of acidity even as the berries ripen to high sugar levels. This results in white wines with both bright acidity and supple texture, a rare and sought-after combination, and one that works perfectly in a transition season like autumn. Furthermore, as you'd imagine from grapes grown on the moon, these wines are austerely fruited and seduce with their minerality and marine salinity. Santorini Assyrtiko is lovely paired with traditional Greek dishes, but in my experience, its finest pairing is risotto, especially a delicate seafood-based version. It has the body to stand up to the dish's creaminess, the acidity to cut through the risotto richness, and the delicate mineral flavors to complement salty seafood.

Space is limited on the island of Santorini. The volcano saw to that. And vine acreage has decreased by half in the past fifty years as vineyards have given way to tourism infrastructure. There are only a handful of Santorini wineries exporting their Assyrtiko to the United States, but do the extra legwork to find them; the wines are exquisite. The volcano saw to that too.

Chianti Classico

September is the perfect time of year to (re)introduce yourself to Chianti Classico, because it is the twilight of peak tomato season, when tomatoes hover between solid and liquid states. Sangiovese has evolved in Tuscan vineyards right alongside the tomatoes that color red the culinary landscape of the region. The high natural acidity of tomatoes makes them devilishly difficult to pair with wine. Many reds will taste flat and insipid next to a fresh marinara sauce. Not so Chianti Classico, which is bursting with its own matching acidity, carrying flavors of sour cherry, strawberry; subtleties of—yep—tomato paste; and, because this is Italy, a comfort level with a certain rustic earthiness and a dash of bitters, like a kiss of Campari to get the blood pumping.

CHIANTI CLASSICO

WHAT	Dry red wine made mostly from the grape variety Sangiovese
WHERE	Tuscany, in central Italy
WHY	Chianti Classico—with its bright acidity and tomato-paste subtleties—is a fantastic red to drink during peak tomato season.
PRONUNCIATION	*kee-YAHN-tee KLA-see-koh*
HOW MUCH	Decent examples cost $20 to $40.
PAIR WITH	A meatball sandwich topped with a mix of provolone, mozzarella, and Parmesan cheeses

DRY LAMBRUSCO

WHAT	Dry, semisparkling red wine made mostly from the grape varieties Lambrusco Sorbara, Lambrusco Grasparossa, and Lambrusco Salamino
WHERE	Mostly in Emilia-Romagna, Italy, between the cities of Parma and Bologna
WHY	This rarity in the wine world—a sparkling red— is the perfect pizza wine: dry, frothy, and refreshing.
PRONUNCIATION	*lahm-BROO-skoh*
HOW MUCH	Decent examples cost $10 to $25.
PAIR WITH	Pizza (anything from thin crust to deep-dish), stromboli, or calzone

Have you tried a proper Chianti Classico recently? (To be clear, watching noted serial killer and aspiring sommelier Hannibal Lecter offer Chianti pairing advice in *The Silence of the Lambs* does not count.) Chianti occupies this odd space where almost everyone has heard of it but few people have actually tasted it. At least not lately.

Tuscan producers exported oceans of the stuff to the States in the 1970s and 1980s, with many of the bottles nestled into those little straw flasks—as essential to midrange Italian-American restaurants of that era as red-and-white-checkered tablecloths, Sinatra blasting from tinny speakers, and mozzarella-stick appetizers for the kids. Do you know the word for that straw flask in Italian? *Fiasco*, which is a near-to-perfect description of much of the juice inside. Let's just say the United States export market was not receiving the very best wine Tuscany had to offer.

Over the subsequent decades, Chianti quality has improved dramatically, but many Americans' views of the wine are anchored to the thin swill of yesteryear. The good news: that also puts an anchor on pricing, and these days, good Chianti can represent outstanding value. The best place to focus is on Chianti Classico, the ancestral heart of Chianti (first geographically defined by a Medici edict in 1716) and the world capital of Sangiovese. This small region runs from Florence in the north to Siena in the south, along a road stained red with grapes and tomatoes.

Dry Lambrusco

"What is your favorite pizza wine" is a question I get asked from time to time. "Beer" is my go-to response, and after the ~~uproarious~~ polite laughter subsides a few ~~minutes~~ seconds later, the questioner is often like: "But seriously." Then I have to put my serious wine professional hat on and give my serious answer, which is an unserious wine: dry Lambrusco. But not old-school 1970s/'80s import Lambrusco. That stuff was sweetened into oblivion for the American Coca-Cola palate. I'm talking about dry, juicy, lightly sparkling, slightly bitter red wine, served chilled. If you want something with the acid to cut through tomato sauce, with the bubbles to scrape melty mozzarella cheese from your palate, and with the character to stand up to the abominations that dot the landscape of American pizza menus, Lambrusco is your huckleberry.

A decent rule of thumb for Italy: if a region is better known for wine than food, expect to pay top dollar for the wine. If a region is better known for food than wine, expect to find serious value. An example of the latter: Emilia-Romagna. Many of the best-loved foods of Italy come from here. *Parmigiano-Reggiano. Prosciutto di Parma. Balsamico di Modena. Lasagne alla Bolognese.* All products of this region. It's an embarrassment of riches. Denizens of this swath of northern Italy eat as well as anyone in the world. But what do they drink?

Oftentimes, Lambrusco, which pairs with a whole host of foods (not just pizza!), including some that are traditionally difficult matches (hard cheeses like Parm-Reg, cured meats like prosciutto). Because Lambruscos are so dynamic with food, people outside of Italy who love to cook (or even just love to eat) are easily smitten as well. Lambrusco is squarely in comeback mode, already gaining toeholds on restaurant wine lists. And it makes sense: good Lambrusco's profile—dry, red, sparkling—is close to unique in wine and opens up all sorts of food-matching possibilities.

These bottles can be confusing. There are four separate Lambrusco regions in Emilia-Romagna and nearly a dozen different grape varieties. All the subregions and varieties begin with the word *Lambrusco,* and they all may or may not end up printed on the wine label. Worse yet, rare is the Lambrusco label that tells you whether the wine inside is dry or Dr Pepper–sweet. It's one of those categories where asking questions at your trusted restaurant or retailer of choice is a very good idea—the payoff will over-deliver on your effort output.

Wine in Restaurants

I could tell you how to order wine the next time you go out to a restaurant, without knowing what that restaurant's wine list looks like. I could also tell you how to navigate the Northwest Passage without charts. Both endeavors are based on profound ignorance, both doomed to catastrophic failure.

There's too much variability. Some restaurants have great servers who you should trust to steer you in the right direction; others have servers who at best don't care about wine and at worst have been asked to push slow-moving bottles on unsuspecting rubes. Some restaurants have clearly communicated lists, separated by regions and price points; others have lists designed to confuse and obfuscate, organized by obscure adjectives (limpid! wanton!). Some restaurants see wine as an important complement to their food, others as profit driver.

Rather than offering tips on what to do in restaurants, allow me to offer a series of don'ts based on hard-earned experience:

Don't order the second-least-expensive wine on the list. The restaurant knows your trick! That slot, well loved by many a thrifty diner who doesn't want to look *that* cheap, is home to the highest profit margin on any smart restaurateur's wine list. That means it's the worst value.

Don't order wine by the glass. Ordering wine in restaurants is generally a lousy value proposition. Ordering by the glass is atrocious. Typical restaurant rule of thumb: the by-the-glass price on the menu is the same price the restaurant paid. *For the entire bottle!*

Come to think of it, *don't buy wine at the restaurant, period*. Bring your own. I mean, be smart about it. Find out the price of "corkage" ahead of time. This is the surcharge a restaurant will tack on for allowing you to bring in your own bottle. It covers stemware, service, and some variable amount depending on how much the restaurant wants to disincentivize BYOB. It's often as little as $10, and restaurant wine pricing is typically about double retail. So if you have a $40 wine budget for the evening, you'd be better off spending it on retail wine ($30) plus corkage ($10) than on the restaurant list (where you'll pay $40 for a wine that would have cost you $20 at retail).

September Meal

Tomato Faux-rata Salad and Fusilli with Tomato Ragù

THE RECOLLECTED IGNORANCE OF CHILDHOOD

I can no longer remember why I ate my first great tomato. But I do remember where, and I do remember when. It was at Smitty's Clam Bar in Somers Point, New Jersey. It was late August, mid-adolescence, the end of one of our family vacations "down the shore." I'm certain I was in a moody funk, because the days of bodysurfing and beach reading and fried seafood were at an end, about to give way to school and homework and sensible meals.

But one more meal on the way out of town, and I ordered a deviled crab cake sandwich: essentially a deep-fried crab croquette dropped onto a buttered bun. The toppings were simple: a swath of tartar sauce and a thick slice of tomato, ruby-red and glistening. Why didn't I take the tomato off? Up until that point, I was utterly convinced of my dislike of tomatoes. Early in my childhood, I had tasted them on winter hoagies, thin-sliced and watery, closer to white than to red, devoid of flavor. At least the lettuce on hoagies had textural crunch to recommend it. Tomatoes seemed like some kind of dullard garnish. They weren't for me. I always took them off.

But not this time. I have to believe that I was first swayed by the aesthetic: the red-to-the-core color, the juices bursting forth and intermingling with the tartar, the sweet-and-savory smell of the thing. So I left the tomato on, I took a bite, and my life was changed.

The recollected ignorance of childhood is painful. I think back now to my aunt and uncle making simple late-summer tomato salads—tomatoes grown in their own garden, paper-thin onions, olive oil and red wine vinegar, salt and pepper—and I remember with a face-palm how I probably chose a bowl of Campbell's tomato soup instead.

It took me many years, and many meals, to understand the difference between tomatoes grown for flavor and tomatoes grown for transport. The latter look beautiful in a grocery-store pyramid, but that beauty literally only goes skin-deep. The most flavorful tomatoes are thin skinned and delicate, their juices threatening to burst forth at any jostle. They're made for home gardens and short-haul farmers' markets.

Tomatoes are intensely seasonal. They ripen to deliciousness in late summer, and by early autumn, they're spent. That short window of peak eating is a feature, not a bug; the ephemerality heightens the pleasure. By the time September rolls around each year, I still find myself occasionally in a moody funk, just like when I was a kid, but now it's the end of tomato season that brings me down. In my childhood, my dad would always bust me out of my depression by suggesting one last round of miniature golf before the school year started. These days, I engage in self-care: one last frenzy of tomato cookery before we set another season aside.

Tomato Faux-rata Salad

I love a proper tomato burrata salad. A lobe of burrata (an outer shell of fresh mozzarella containing a gooey core of cream-soaked curds) is a subtle, creamy counterpoint to sweetly acidic ripe tomatoes. But sourcing burrata is a hit-or-miss proposition, so this recipe cheats a little, creating a fake burrata using ingredients that are more broadly available.

The type of tomato is less important here than its ripeness. Grab whichever heirlooms or beefsteaks look the most like water balloons and slice as carefully as you can.

Makes 4 servings

½ cup whole milk ricotta cheese

1 tablespoon whipping cream

1 teaspoon freshly squeezed lemon juice

¼ teaspoon finely grated lemon zest

Kosher salt

1 (8-ounce) ball fresh mozzarella

1½ pounds ripe tomatoes

Freshly cracked black pepper

3 tablespoons extra-virgin olive oil

12 leaves fresh basil ▶

Prepare the ricotta. In a medium bowl, whisk together the ricotta, whipping cream, lemon juice, and lemon zest. Season to taste with salt and set aside.

Create the faux-rata. Drain the mozzarella ball and slice it nearly in half, leaving a thin connection at the bottom of the ball. Set the split ball at the center of a large serving plate and fill the opening with the ricotta mixture. You can be decadent and use it all, or set some aside. (It makes a wonderful dessert when served along fresh fruit for dipping.)

Prepare the tomatoes. For the prettiest slices, place each tomato on its side and cut slices, approximately ¼ inch thick, from bottom to top. I prefer a serrated knife for the task (a sharp bread knife will work great); if you're using a chef's knife, it needs to be ridiculously sharp or you'll end up popping the water balloon. Arrange the slices in an overlapping circle around the faux-rata.

Garnish and serve. Season the tomatoes with salt (recall that you've already seasoned the faux-rata) and pepper. Drizzle the olive oil generously over the tomatoes and cheese. Tear the basil leaves into small pieces and sprinkle them over everything. Serve family style, allowing your guests to grab their favorite tomatoes along with a spoonful of faux-rata.

Fusilli
with Tomato Ragù

Fresh fusilli is more a suggestion than a rule here. Any short pasta (fresh or dried) with nooks and crannies for holding a sauce will work great; rotini, gemelli, or campanelle are all outstanding choices.

Again, I'm not dogmatic on the type of tomato; it's the ripeness that's essential. Sometimes the green heirlooms are at peak, and this ragù turns a deep shade of emerald. Other times the reds and yellows shine, and the sauce turns sunset-orange. Any color will look beautiful if the flavor is good. If you happen to be making this outside of fresh tomato season, it's better to substitute good canned whole tomatoes than to work with underripe "fresh" tomatoes.

A few years ago, I started ignoring calls in recipes to peel and seed tomatoes. I've never gone back. The seeds add a little crunch, the skins toothsome texture. Leaving seeds and skins makes for more rustic dishes, and that's fine by me, especially considering the added benefit of huge time savings.

Makes 4 servings

2 tablespoons extra-virgin olive oil

1 large sweet onion, roughly chopped

Kosher salt

½ pound hot Italian sausage, casings removed

4 cloves garlic, finely chopped

¾ cup dry white wine, such as Sauvignon Blanc or Chardonnay

3 pounds ripe tomatoes, roughly chopped

2 tablespoons whipping cream

1 pound fresh fusilli pasta

Grated Parmigiano-Reggiano cheese, for garnish

Chopped fresh parsley, for garnish

Sauté the sausage. In a large skillet or braising pot over medium-high heat, heat the olive oil, add the onion and a pinch of salt, and cook, stirring occasionally, until soft and golden, about 5 minutes. Add the sausage and cook until it renders fat, then add the garlic and continue cooking until the sausage is browned, breaking it into smaller pieces as it cooks. ▶

Build the sauce. Add the wine, scraping any browned bits from the bottom of the pot. Bring to a boil and boil until the wine has evaporated. Add the tomatoes and cook over medium-high heat, stirring occasionally, until they break down and the sauce thickens, 15 to 20 minutes. (After 5 minutes, the tomatoes should begin to lose their shape and give up their juices. After 10 minutes, you'll have a thin, chunky sauce. By 20 minutes, you should have a nice thick ragù.) Now add the cream, reduce the heat to maintain a simmer, and simmer for 5 minutes. Season with salt to taste, and keep warm over low heat.

Cook the pasta. In a large saucepan over high heat, bring 4 quarts of salted water to a boil. Add the fusilli, reduce the heat to medium-high, and cook at a gentle boil until al dente (with fresh pasta, I begin checking 90 seconds after the water returns to a boil, with the overall cooking time usually between 2 and 4 minutes). Just before draining, add ½ cup pasta cooking water to the ragù. Drain the pasta and stir it into the ragù.

Serve. I like to serve this pasta in broad, deep bowls with a generous pile of Parmigiano-Reggiano and a pinch of parsley atop each one.

Substitutions and Notes: Any fresh or dried pasta can work in place of fusilli. Mild Italian sausage is fine in place of hot if you'd prefer less heat.

Pairing: Chianti Classico has evolved in Tuscany to pair with that tomato-based cuisine, and it is the nonpareil choice with this meal.

ALTO ADIGE PINOT BIANCO

WHAT	Dry white wine made from the grape variety Pinot Bianco
WHERE	Northern Italy, along the alpine border with Austria and Switzerland
WHY	This part of Italy is producing a series of drastically underpriced white wines, and Pinot Bianco may be the best of the bunch.
PRONUNCIATION	*al-toh AH-dee-zhay pee-noh bee-YAHN-ko*
HOW MUCH	Decent examples cost $15 to $25.
PAIR WITH	Roasted chicken thighs nestled onto soft polenta

Alto Adige Pinot Bianco

Alto Adige is rapidly emerging as one of the world's great sources of white wine values. Sited at a crossroads of cultural influences, it is a garden where a seemingly endless number of flowers blossom into splendor. Blooms from Italy via Pinot Grigio; Austria via Grüner Veltliner; France via Chardonnay, Sauvignon Blanc (here simply called Sauvignon), and Gewürztraminer; Germany via Riesling, Kerner, Sylvaner, and Müller-Thurgau. All labeled varietally, all easy to understand, all kissed with alpine freshness.

My favorite of all the Alto Adige whites is a dramatically underappreciated late bloomer, one grown in all four of the aforementioned countries but truly claimed by none of them. In Austria and Germany, it is called Weissburgunder; in France, Pinot Blanc. And in Alto Adige, where it reaches its highest expression, it is Pinot Bianco.

This variety is like Wolverine: a persecuted mutant. Pinot Bianco is a genetic mutation of Pinot Noir, and the mutations can happen spontaneously in the vineyard. So you're out there growing Pinot Noir, and you're walking your vineyard rows, and all your grapes are red, and then out of the corner of your eye you notice one cane of one vine with white grapes: delicious freak of nature Pinot Bianco. Propagate that cane throughout an entire vineyard, and you have yourself a field of Pinot Bianco.

The grape is an underdog through and through. In the vineyard, it is frequently confused with Chardonnay (the two varieties are nearly identical to look at). Its genetic freak sister Pinot Grigio garners *waaaaay* more attention (and sales) despite its oft-snoozeworthy alcoholic apple juice profile. In many other regions, Bianco is seen as a high-yielding workhorse, offering a dependably cheap blending partner for entry-level bottlings. But grown here, at alpine elevation, the grape is transformed, combining the best aspects of Chardonnay (textural weight and character) and Pinot Grigio (bright acidity and accessible pricing). The result is a seductive autumn white with the weight to stand up to the richer dishes that land on fall tables, and with evocative floral/leafy aromatics, something like chamomile tea, to complement a core of creamy citrus and stone fruit.

When you grow up in Philadelphia, as I did, you learn to love an underdog (a less charitable interpretation would be that you learn to root for losers). Pinot Bianco from this part of the world is still very much a loveworthy underdog, but one showing signs of a Cinderella run in the offing.

Central Otago Pinot Noir

Only a handful of regions are capable of producing compelling Pinot Noir. Pinot isn't like most of the other sun- and fun-loving varieties. Pinot is the pale goth kid who sunburns easily and would rather be reading a book on a rainy day than cannonballing at a pool party. It's thin skinned, delicate. It thrives in marginal climates. Most of the New World regions succeeding with Pinot Noir have been doing so for only a very short period of time. Put simply, the prevailing wisdom in these regions for many decades was: the weather is too damned miserable to grow much of anything here.

That was true for Oregon Pinot Noir (see page 64), whose industry didn't emerge in earnest until the 1970s. And it's true for New Zealand's Central Otago, source of some of the most exciting Pinot from any region, New World or Old, and all from an industry that is barely three decades old. At first blush, you can't blame the Kiwis for taking some time to unlock this region's potential. Central Otago is seriously far to the south. Certainly the southernmost winegrowing region in New Zealand, it competes with Patagonia in Argentina for southernmost winegrowing region in the world. As in, close-to-Antarctica south.

Every great Pinot Noir–producing region seems to require not only a marginal climate but at least one additional major obstacle. Burgundy has hail. Oregon has autumn rains. And Central Otago has . . . well . . . bunny rabbits. Okay, I know what you're thinking: Bunnies? They're so cute and cuddly! And they bring physiologically-questionable-yet-undeniably-delicious eggs around Easter time!

CENTRAL OTAGO PINOT NOIR

WHAT	Dry red wine made from the grape variety Pinot Noir
WHERE	The South Island of New Zealand
WHY	This young (three-decade) Pinot-growing region is showing enormous potential, and prices haven't yet caught up to quality.
PRONUNCIATION	*oh-TA-go pee-noh nwahr*
HOW MUCH	Decent examples cost $20 to $40.
PAIR WITH	Sweet-and-salty teriyaki salmon

MADEIRA

WHAT	Off-dry to sweet fortified wine made mostly from the grape varieties Sercial, Verdelho, Bual, and Malmsey
WHERE	The island of Madeira, west of Morocco in the Atlantic Ocean
WHY	The Founding Fathers loved Madeira, and this caramel-kissed sweet wine is still wonderful today, especially next to a plate of salty cheeses.
PRONUNCIATION	*mah-DAY-ruh*
HOW MUCH	Decent examples cost $20 to $40 for 375-milliliter or 500-milliliter bottles.
PAIR WITH	The nicest hunk of Manchego cheese you can find

Not these bunnies. Introduced to New Zealand in the early nineteenth century as food source and hunting sport, they quickly took over, especially in Central Otago, which is blanketed in grand cru rabbit grasses. With an ample, delicious food supply in place, the rabbits did what rabbits do so well: multiply. The scourge has reached the point where there is now an annual Easter Bunny Hunt (no lie) that takes out as many as ten thousand rabbits in a single day.

What does this have to do with Pinot Noir? In addition to overgrazing Otago's perfect grass (which causes erosion and leaves less food for the region's sheep), rabbits also enjoy the trunks of grapevines. Fortunately, Otago winemakers have mitigated the rabbit problem via robust fences, and the region continues on its upward ascendancy with Pinot Noir, which here retains the rugged sense of earthiness that makes Pinot Noir from Burgundy so appealing, paired to succulent, openly delicious red fruit. Otago Pinot's earthy subtleties are those of leaves and mushrooms and soil, perfect for autumn, the season of benevolent decay. The best versions evoke twilight walks on darkening trails, leaves crunching underfoot and winter giving chase.

Madeira

A bill from Philadelphia's City Tavern, after a party during the Constitutional Convention in 1787, contained the following beverages: sixty bottles Bordeaux, twenty-two bottles porter, twelve bottles beer, eight bottles cider, eight bottles whiskey, seven bowls punch. And fifty-four bottles Madeira. Do you want to know how many delegates attended the party? Are you thinking it must be a number in the hundreds? The actual number is fifty-five. Yes, that's one bottle of Madeira per attendee (the designated buggy driver abstained).

Despite its origin on a Portuguese island several thousand miles east of Philadelphia, Madeira is a wine intractably bound up in American history.

For many sailors in the age of exploration, the island was the last port of call before heading for the Americas, the last chance to provision with booze for the rollicking trip ahead. To keep the wine from spoiling during the trip, Madeira winemakers fortified their wines with a neutral spirit. What happened after that was unexpected.

Onboard the ships, the barrels heated up as they traveled through tropical climes, and the wine inside sloshed around, exposing it to oxygen. Both the heat and the oxygenation profoundly transformed the wines. By the time they arrived at their ports of call, the Madeiras possessed a mix of sweet fresh and cooked fruits, spiced nuts, and caramelized notes like browned butter. Denizens of the American colonies couldn't get enough of the stuff, and for some time, winemakers in Madeira didn't even realize the process was happening. (International text messaging was still about two centuries off.) It wasn't until the Madeirans received back some unsold round-tripped wine that they became aware of the benevolent adulterations transforming their wines.

Modern Madeira producers don't send barrels off in ships, but their production process (called *estufagem*) replicates the effect by exposing the barrels to limited amounts of oxygen and storing them in warm upstairs rooms left to heat (or *maderize*). These days, vintage Madeira (especially from older vintages) can be extremely expensive. Instead, look for the best value in blends of multiple vintages, labeled as "5 Year" or "10 Year."

All the wines have some residual sugar, the range running from Sercial (the driest) to Verdelho to Bual to Malmsey. The wines at the drier end of the range are lovely as aperitifs and are the best of the bunch to use for cooking, tailor-made to elevate autumn's mushroom bounty onto a higher plane. Take your best chicken Marsala or coq au vin recipe and replace the recipes' wines with Sercial Madeira. Cue groans of pleasure.

All the grapes grown on Madeira retain outstanding natural acidity, which helps to keep the finished wines from being too overtly sweet or cloying, even those at the richest end. Those sweeter Buals and Malmseys are perfect pairings for an after-dinner cheese plate or quiet post prandial contemplation of your pocket Constitution.

Does Vintage Matter?

The vast majority of wines include the vintage year someplace on their label. This is the year the grapes were harvested, grapes eventually fermented into the wine you're considering whether to pick up off the shelf. Does vintage matter? Is this a part of the label to which you should pay careful attention?

It depends. And what it depends on are the goals of the winery in question. At a broad level, wineries can be split into two camps: those whose goal is consistency, and those whose goal is expressiveness.

Wineries aiming for consistency usually produce bottles that end up on the bottom shelves of our local wine shops. These are wines that cost $3 to $15, and they attract wine drinkers who don't want to overthink their purchases. They'll reach for the same label every time, and in exchange for that loyalty, the winery does everything in its power to make sure the wine tastes the same each time, no matter the year the grapes were harvested. For these wines, vintage really does not matter, because this is wine-as-commodity. You wouldn't ask to see the year the wheat was harvested in your box of Ritz Crackers; why would you care about the harvest date of the grapes in your wine?

Moving up the price ladder, we find more wineries that value expressiveness. They don't view wine as a commodity but instead as a unique agricultural product that can express the specific place where it was grown and the specific season in which it was grown. If it was a cool year, with less-ripe grapes, the finished wines will have lower alcohol and higher acidity; warmer-year wines will contain riper fruit and softer texture. For these wineries, vintage does indeed matter; the same wine from the same winery across different vintages can taste vastly different. The best resource for information about vintages is likely your local retail steward, but there are also a number of online vintage guides from national publications like *Wine Spectator* and *Wine Advocate*.

If you're reading this right now and thinking, *Seriously? Isn't wine complicated enough? Now I have to learn about the hailstorms in Barolo in 2014?* picture me nodding sympathetically but also giving you some straight talk, which is that many wine lovers are willing to embrace this kind of vintage minutiae and forego consistency because it is exactly the variability of wine—the fact that it is a living product from a specific window in time—that makes it such a uniquely thrilling drink.

October Meal

Sluggard's Polenta with Sercial-Spiked Lobster Mushrooms and Brazilian-Style Collard Greens

CONSIDER THE LOBSTER

There you are, casually negotiating pizza toppings with your friends. Someone blithely mentions mushrooms. Heads nod around the room. Universal approval. Does a single member of the party stop and think this through? Is there a woke millennial in the house who can pause and consider that the group is about to call a fine pizzeria dining establishment and ask the proprietors and their employees to—on purpose—place on top of their steaming tomato-and-cheese pie dozens of chunks of the fleshy fruiting body of a fungus?

That we consume mushrooms at all is objectively disgusting. This is the fungus kingdom. You know what else lives in the fungus kingdom? That growth on your big toe that is days away from making the nail fall off. The mildew creeping up your shower curtain like an advancing late-afternoon shadow. You're not asking Domino's to sprinkle either of those next to your pepperoni, are you?

And yet. Mushrooms are pretty damned tasty.

They fit into a human pattern where we don't often consider what we as a society have deemed edible and what we have deemed gross. I mean, lobsters? Seriously? We cook them up and peel off their exoskeletons and dip them into melted butter and that's okay? But cockroach scampi is gross? What's the difference?

Now consider the lobster mushroom, my favorite fungus of them all. It's even worse. It's one parasitic fungus (*Hypomyces lactifluorum*) invading another wholly innocent fungus (usually *Russula*) and taking control of the organism. Like Kuato from *Total Recall*. (The original 1990 Schwarzenegger film, not the 2012 Colin Farrell abomination.) Parasite plus fungus seems like an unlikely equation for delicious, but there you have it.

And this is one seriously beneficial parasite. It takes a mushroom that is edible but entirely boring and completely transforms it. The color becomes a blaze of reddish orange, not unlike a lobster. The flavor becomes complex: nutty and briny and earthy in turn, not unlike a lobster. And the texture becomes succulent and toothsome, not unlike—okay, you get the point: it was an easy mushroom to name.

In October I'm hungry for all sorts of mushrooms. There's something about the cool crepuscular air, about leaves falling back to earth and making new soil, that makes me crave these dirty wonders. If you've limited your mushroom intake mostly to buttons and creminis and the occasional chanterelle, you owe it to yourself to consider the lobster.

Sluggard's Polenta

with Sercial-Spiked Lobster Mushrooms and Brazilian-Style Collard Greens

I like to feature lobster mushrooms by placing them atop a subtle, creamy bowl of polenta. Polenta too is perfectly autumnal, its corn flavor a memory of summertime, its porridge texture a preview of the colder months to come.

And let's get this out of the way right now. I never make polenta on the stovetop anymore, and neither should you. Let the restaurant professionals who are paid hourly tackle that forearm-destroying task. You can use the sluggard's oven method and then take all that extra time to work on the mushrooms. Or catch up on a movie. Perhaps *Total Recall*.

Makes 4 servings

1 cup coarsely ground yellow cornmeal
3 cups water
2 cups whole milk
3 tablespoons unsalted butter, divided

Kosher salt
Sercial-Spiked Lobster Mushrooms (recipe follows)

Brazilian-Style Collard Greens (recipe follows)
Chopped fresh parsley, for garnish

▶

Prepare the polenta. Preheat the oven to 350 degrees F. In a large heavy-bottomed pot, whisk together the cornmeal, water, milk, and 2 tablespoons of the butter. Place the pot in the oven, uncovered, and bake for 45 minutes. Stir once and bake for an additional 15 minutes, then stir and check every 5 minutes until the polenta reaches the desired creamy consistency, usually 65 to 75 minutes total. Whisk in 1 more tablespoon of the butter and season with salt to taste.

Serve. Spoon the polenta into large, shallow bowls. Top one half of each bowl with a generous serving of mushrooms and the other half with collard greens. Garnish with parsley.

Sercial-Spiked Lobster Mushrooms

The natural nuttiness of lobster mushrooms cries out for a preparation that enhances that aspect, and I almost always choose a nutty deglazing alcohol to do the trick. Sometimes it's Amontillado or Oloroso Sherry; sometimes it's even a nut-based spirit like Frangelico. But my favorite lately has been Madeira, and specifically Sercial, the driest category of Madeira. Sercial has just the right mix of nut and caramel notes, without an excess of sugar to make the dish cloying.

Makes 4 servings

3 tablespoons unsalted butter	4 cloves garlic, minced	1 cup chicken stock
1 pound lobster mushrooms, cleaned with a dry brush and cut into medium dice	1 tablespoon chopped fresh thyme	¼ cup whipping cream
	2 teaspoons all-purpose flour	Kosher salt
	½ cup Sercial Madeira	

Sauté the mushrooms. In a large skillet over medium-high heat, melt 3 tablespoons butter, then add the mushrooms and sauté until tender and beginning to brown, 6 to 8 minutes. Add the garlic and thyme and cook until fragrant, 1 to 2 minutes. Add the flour, stir to coat the mushrooms, and cook for 1 more minute. ▶

Glaze the mushrooms. Add the Madeira and deglaze the pan, scraping up any browned bits. Boil until the liquid is mostly evaporated and a glaze develops on the mushrooms. Add the stock and cream, return to a boil, then lower to a simmer and cook for 5 minutes. Season with salt to taste.

Brazilian-Style Collard Greens *(Couve à Mineira)*

Most of the collard greens consumed in this country are braised or boiled into porky oblivion. Nothing wrong with that. But there is another way. And it's a much, much faster way. By slicing collards into thin strips and then sautéing them hot and fast with olive oil and garlic, they retain their bright-green vibrancy, their natural toothsome bite, and their pleasing, subtle bitter tones, which serve as beautiful counterpoints to an otherwise rich plate of food.

Makes 4 servings

1 pound collard greens	4 cloves garlic, minced
1 tablespoon extra-virgin olive oil	Kosher salt
	Juice from 1 small lemon

Prepare the greens. Remove the stem from each large leaf, and then, in batches of 4 to 6 leaves, roll them tightly into a cigar shape and slice crosswise into thin strips.

Sauté the greens. In a large skillet over medium heat, heat the olive oil, then add the garlic and a pinch of salt. Cook until the garlic is golden and fragrant, about 2 minutes. Add the collards and cook, stirring frequently, until they take on a bright-green color and are crisp-tender, about 4 minutes. Season with salt and lemon juice to taste.

Substitutions and Notes: Leftover polenta makes for an incredible brunch topped with crisp bacon and two fried eggs. If lobster mushrooms aren't available, other wild mushrooms (chanterelles especially) will work great; so too creminis and buttons. Don't use any Madeira sweeter than Sercial; if Sercial isn't available, aim instead for a dry Sherry or a dry white wine. As a substitute for collard greens, other leafy greens like kale or Swiss chard also take to this preparation beautifully.

Pairing: Earthy, vibrant Pinot Noir is a classic pairing with any dish involving mushrooms. Use a Central Otago Pinot Noir with this meal to see why.

CHABLIS

WHAT	Dry white wine made from the grape variety Chardonnay
WHERE	The northern edge of Burgundy in central France
WHY	Real Chablis (not the bottom-shelf jug wine) is bone dry, steely, and flinty, and among the most exciting expressions of Chardonnay available.
PRONUNCIATION	*sha-BLEE*
HOW MUCH	Decent examples cost $20 to $30.
PAIR WITH	Shallow-fried pork cutlets, either katsu-style or schnitzel-style

Chablis

There it sits, fat and ponderous, on the bottom shelf of the grocery store wine section. A squat, 1.5-liter glass jug, with a small ring for finger-hooking leverage, and small font on the label that reads "100 Percent Grape Wine" (you'd like to think that would be presupposed). In large font, the label reads "Chablis," which is an alternative fact at best, a bald-faced lie at worst. We Americans have perpetrated a number of wine atrocities over the years, but calling semisweet Central Valley California anonymous white wine "Chablis" has to be among the worst.

Real Chablis comes from the region of Chablis in France. Similarities to the jug-wine funhouse-mirror doppelgangers begin and end with the fact that both wines are white. After that, it's all difference. Real Chablis is bone dry, steely, and flinty, made entirely with Chardonnay grown in Burgundy's coldest, most northerly outpost. What separates Chablis from the rest of Burgundy is its soil. The entire region used to be part of an ancient seabed, covered in mollusks. Today, vines dig into plots of earth lousy with marine fossils, making wines that pair perfectly with the descendants of those ancient crustaceans. This is the most mineral expression of Chardonnay in the world, beautiful with rich winter seafood like lobster and crab. Put briny cold-water chopped clams on top of a simple winter pizza with garlic and herbs and cheese, and you have Chablis-pairing perfection.

As much as jug Chablis pains the wine purist in me, my cheapskate side offers a small round of applause, because doubtless the brand confusion sown by the bottom-shelf jugs has kept Chablis from the top-shelf pricing commanded by its white Burgundy kin. Trying to purchase most white Burgundy is an exercise in chasing dragons. Those brave (foolish?) enough to go hunting are in rare cases rewarded with gold and jewels. More frequently they're rewarded with a mouthful of fiery Smaug breath in the form of underwhelming, wallet-reaving Meursault or Puligny-Montrachet.

Chablis is a different story. It is the northern satellite to Burgundy, the dot to the region's lowercase *i* shape, and closer geographically to Champagne than to Burgundy proper. The out-of-the-way location further contributes to Chablis retaining moderate pricing compared to top-tier white Burg. Yes, good Premier Cru and Grand Cru Chablis prices can run well into three digits, but opt instead for wine labeled "Chablis AOC" (*appellation d'origine contrôlée*, the French term describing a demarcated region known for producing specific agricultural products, like wines). For $20, this basic Chablis (100 percent grape wine; I guarantee it) can offer a full winter evening of quiet contemplation.

Langhe Rosso

Everything tastes better on vacation. But why? Some of it is certainly the "oddball effect" popularized by neuroscientist David Eagleman, which says that when your brain is experiencing new impulses (oddballs), it slows your sense of time down, and you experience them more fully. He proved this effect by asking subjects to watch a series of flashing images—mostly a brown shoe, occasionally a flower—and report how long each image lingered on the screen. His marks consistently concluded that the flowers lingered longer, when in reality each image flashed for the exact same amount of time.

Time, according to Eagleman, "is this rubbery thing. It stretches out when you really turn your brain resources on, and when you say, 'Oh, I got this, everything is as expected,' it shrinks up." In other words, you probably pay more attention to the *fonduta con tartufi* (a melty mix of fontina cheese and white truffles) when you're sitting in a restaurant in the Piedmont because the experience is utterly unfamiliar. The mac and cheese you make every Wednesday, the one that most certainly does not contain white truffles: that your mind barely notices anymore.

In all likelihood, the wine that was served next to the *fonduta*, the one that was probably poured out of a large pitcher and into a small flat glass that didn't really allow for swirling and sniffing but instead seemed expressly designed to complement the food, that wine was a Langhe Rosso.

LANGHE ROSSO

WHAT	Dry red blend made mostly from Nebbiolo, Dolcetto, and Barbera grapes
WHERE	Piedmont, in northwestern Italy near the alpine border with France
WHY	These blends of Nebbiolo, Dolcetto, and Barbera are vinified unfussily and offer food-friendly rusticity, early drinking character, and easy-on-the-wallet pricing.
PRONUNCIATION	*LAN-gay ROH-soh*
HOW MUCH	Decent examples cost $15 to $25.
PAIR WITH	Braised pot roast with lots of cremini mushrooms

And if that drinking experience is also difficult to replicate at home, well, it's not just the oddball effect; it's also that the wine is difficult to find at home.

The Langhe is a region bursting with beautiful wines. It contains Barolo and Barbaresco, both made from the noble Nebbiolo grape. It contains fruity-delicious Dolcetto d'Alba and lip-smacking Barbera d'Asti. And, since 1994, it has contained a beautiful catchall category: Langhe Rosso.

Langhe DOC (*denominazione di origine controllata*, a controlled appellation in Italy) was established in the mid-'90s to give winemakers room to experiment with varieties not traditional to the region (hence Langhe Chardonnay became a popular category) or to declassify lots that didn't quite make the cut for Barolo and Barbaresco (these became Langhe Nebbiolo). But it also allowed for Langhe Rosso, a broad category that contains varietal wines and blends, but which has turned out to most often be a blend of Langhe's traditional red trinity: Nebbiolo, Dolcetto, and Barbera.

These blends—popular locally—have taken time to build import momentum in the United States, I suspect because Langhe producers thought it would be better to focus initially on varietal wines, which are easier for the American consumer to understand. But Langhe Rosso blends are phenomenal, a classic case of a whole wine being stronger than the sum of its parts. Nebbiolo brings its haunting tar-and-roses aromatics and its robust structure, Barbera a lightning bolt of pie-cherry and blood-orange acidity, Dolcetto rich grapey pleasure—but the overall package is something more, something lithe and leafy and perfect for autumn. It has become a go-to on my Thanksgiving table every year, a beautiful, versatile wine that will slow time down for anyone who drinks it.

Spotting Common Wine Faults and Flaws

There are bad wines—these tend to be out of balance in one way or another: flabby (not enough acid) or sharp (too much acid), astringent (too much tannin) or insipid (not enough tannin), hot (too much alcohol) or thin (not enough alcohol)—and then there are wines that are faulty or flawed in some way. If you purchase the former, you're out of luck; throw it into the cooking pot or serve it to your frenemies. If you purchase the latter, you may have some recourse. Here's how to spot the most common wine problems.

Cork taint. Smells like: wet, musty, moldering cardboard. Comes from: trichloroanisole (TCA), a compound that turns up from time to time in natural cork. TCA does not do anything physical to the cork, so examining the cork won't give you any clues; it's all in the aromatics and the muting effect on the taste of the wine.

Reduction. Smells like: sulfurous notes of egg or lit matchstick. Comes from: volatile sulfur compounds, usually a result of the wine not being exposed to enough oxygen during the winemaking process. This will often blow off as the wine is exposed to more oxygen, so swirl what's in your glass vigorously, and bust out the old decanter for the remainder of the bottle.

Oxidation. Smells like: fresh or roasted nuts, Sherry. Comes from: overexposure to oxygen during the winemaking process, or a failed cork after bottling. Color is also a dead giveaway here. Just like a cut apple will turn brown with oxygen exposure, so too will an oxidized wine, with both whites and reds taking on noticeable browning shades.

Cooked. Smells like: cooked or baked fruit instead of fresh fruit. Comes from: exposure, usually after bottling, to excessive heat. If you're at a restaurant that stores their wines on the highest shelves possible, be on the smellout for cooked bottles.

Volatile acidity. Smells like: vinegar, nail-polish remover. Comes from: bacteria, common to wine, which produce acetic acid, the acid that gives vinegar its signature tang. No amount of swirling or decanting will mitigate this particular issue.

Brett. Smells like: a Band-Aid or a barnyard. Comes from: *Brettanomyces*, a yeast that turns up occasionally in vineyards and wineries. Some drinkers like a touch of brett in their wine and the funky/earthy complexities it can bring, but any more than a very little and you wind up squarely in manure-wine territory.

TAVEL ROSÉ

WHAT	Dry Rosé made mostly from Grenache and Cinsault
WHERE	The Southern Rhône Valley in southern France
WHY	Tavel produces only one type of wine—Rosé—and the specialty of the region is a darker, richer, fuller style of Rosé perfect for winter in general, and Thanksgiving especially.
PRONUNCIATION	*ta-vel ro-ZAY*
HOW MUCH	Decent examples cost $15 to $25.
PAIR WITH	Anything involving crispy pork belly or bacon

Tavel Rosé

The Rosé wave currently swamping American shores—influenced heavily by the wines of Provence—is composed almost entirely of light-bodied, crisp wines with a series of pink hues so pale and delicate that a strong squint is required to confirm that no, you did not mistakenly pull a bottle of white out of the fridge. But just sixty miles to the northwest of Aix-en-Provence is Tavel, the longtime capital of a very different type of Rosé: rich, full-bodied, and supply textured, with darker fruits like black cherries and blackberries and shades of pink more often seen on Hello Kitty's hair bows.

These are the Rosés for the long dark of winter, and these are the Rosés for Thanksgiving. I have a few rules for Thanksgiving wine. One is moderate alcohol: you want to be buzzed enough to hear Uncle Bruce's political opinions without losing your mind, but you don't want to be passed out before the cranberry sauce slithers out of the can. Tavel, by law, cannot exceed 13.5 percent alcohol. Check.

The most important rule is versatility. Have you seen the horrors of the Thanksgiving table? Dark turkey meat next to green bean casserole; corn bread–sausage stuffing next to sweet potato–marshmallow casserole; Jell-O "salad" (an optimistic term) next to mashed potatoes. Tavel pairs beautifully with this series of culinary abominations, offering just enough palate-cleaning acidity and plenty of heft and weight to stand up to the rich flavors that dot the table.

Tavel is the only region in France solely dedicated to the production of Rosé, and they've been producing wine there for centuries. Tavel wine was famously adored by two French kings (Philip IV in the thirteenth century and Louis XIV in the seventeenth century), a series of popes in nearby Avignon, and, more recently, by a pair of famous American men of letters: Ernest Hemingway, who didn't write much about Tavel but drank plenty of it, and A. J. Liebling, who while drinking Tavel Rosé in Paris in the 1920s described the first glass as "an enthusiasm held under restraint. With the second glass," he continued, "the enthusiasm gains; with the third, it is overpowering."

Leftover Thanksgiving Turkey Schmaltzo Ball Soup with Shaved Beet and Radish Salad

A THANKSGIVUKKAH TRADITION

Do you ever feel like the universe is giving you a sign that it's time to make a change? You know, like when you rear-end the car in front of you while texting a friend about your terrible boss—that's the universe suggesting that you should quit your job. And stop texting while driving. Probably stop driving altogether.

My sign came in autumn 2013, when the specter of Thanksgivukkah first began to loom. I was raised by one secular Jew and one secular gentile, and when we "observed" Hanukkah (and Christmas for that matter), the religiosity of the season was regularly eclipsed by the food. (And the presents.) I felt pretty certain I would have remembered a Thanksgiving/Hanukkah mashup had one taken place during my childhood. As it turns out, it didn't happen during my childhood, nor during anyone else's.

Breathless newscasters were reporting that 2013 was the first ever Thanksgivukkah convergence (not true: it happened in both 1888 and 1899, although to be fair, back then Thanksgiving took place later than the fourth Thursday of November), and that there wouldn't be another convergence until the year 79811 (also not true; there will be brief overlaps—the first night of Hanukkah occurring on the evening of Thanksgiving—in 2070 and 2165).

Despite some exaggerations, the fact remained: the Thanksgivukkah convergence was extraordinary. I saw it as a clear sign. A sign that it was time to unburden my friends and family from the tyranny of the day-after-Thanksgiving leftover turkey sandwich. To give them something better. Something soul-nourishing. Something to put the *ukkah* in Thanksgivukkah.

Leftover Thanksgiving Turkey Schmaltzo Ball Soup

I got too drunk on Thanksgiving night 2013 to remember my grand soup plans. Fortunately, before leaving for the night, my friend Katie put the turkey carcass into our biggest stockpot, poured the leftover gravy on top of it, and added just enough water to cover the bird. Then she slammed a lid on that pot, set it to a simmer, and left.

The next morning, we awoke to a fine layer of turkey condensate on every window of the house. And the shower curtains. I remember that specifically, because our shower became a de facto turkey *shvitz* for weeks after that, which I found appealing but other family members found incomprehensibly abhorrent.

The source of the turkey mist was still bubbling away happily on the stovetop that morning. At that point the vision in my head was turkey matzo ball soup. It wasn't until I was groggily pouring the strained soup into a fat separator that I had one of those precoffee moments of perfect lucidity. I was going to use that schmaltz (yes, I know, *schmaltz* means chicken fat, not turkey fat; when the universe gave me the sign, it also granted a minor Yiddish poultry dispensation) instead of canola oil. I wasn't going to make turkey matzo ball soup. I was going to make turkey *schmaltzo* ball soup.

Makes 8 Black Friday–brunch servings for hungover adults

1 Thanksgiving turkey carcass

Up to 1 cup leftover gravy (optional)

1 pound carrots, roughly chopped

1 pound celery, roughly chopped, leaves reserved for garnish

2 medium yellow onions, peeled and halved

8 large eggs, beaten

¼ cup seltzer water (optional)

2 cups matzo meal

2 teaspoons kosher salt

▶

Prepare the turkey broth. In a large stockpot, gently nestle the turkey carcass, pour in the gravy, and add enough water to just cover the turkey. Bring to a boil over high heat, reduce the heat to a maintain a simmer, and then simmer, uncovered, for at least 6 hours or overnight, taking care not to burn your house down in the process. Remove the carcass (which will now be falling apart) to a large platter and strain the broth through a fine-mesh strainer into a fat separator. Reserve the glistening golden turkey schmaltz (allowing it to cool to room temperature), and return the (mostly) clear broth back to the (mostly) clean stockpot.

Add the aromatics. Add the carrots, celery, and onion to the broth and return to a simmer. Simmer until the vegetables are tender, about 1 hour, then discard the onions. Keep the broth warm over low heat.

Scavenge the turkey. While the vegetables are simmering, use your fingers to pick the remaining meat off the bird, setting it aside for later. (Waiting until the turkey has cooled down is a good idea.) Employing the tiny fingers of children is an even better idea. Turkeys have an impossible number of bones—exponentially more than chickens. Many (tiny) hands make light work.

Prepare the schmaltzo ball mixture. In a large bowl, combine the eggs, ½ cup of the reserved turkey schmaltz, and seltzer if you want extra-fluffy balls. Add the matzo meal and salt. Stir to combine, doing so as gently as possible for lighter, more delicate balls. Refrigerate, uncovered, for 30 minutes.

Form the schmaltzo balls. Two important tips here: First, wet your hands early and often to keep from wearing matzo gloves. Second, do not over-form the balls. Set the obsessive-compulsive part of your personality aside for 15 minutes, take deep cleansing breaths, and be okay with misshapen balls. ▶

That is by far the lesser sin than dense balls, which is what you will wind up with if you overwork the dough into perfect spheres. The target is 1-inch balls (a golf ball is 1.68 inches, for reference), but a little variance is perfectly acceptable. Place the formed balls on a plate lined with wax paper.

Assemble the soup. In a large pot over high heat, bring 2 to 3 quarts of salted water to a boil. Gently lower the balls into the water, reduce the heat to maintain a simmer, cover, and simmer until tender, about 30 minutes. Meanwhile, add the picked turkey meat to the stockpot of broth, and bring it back up to a bare simmer. When the schmaltzo balls are finished simmering, transfer them with a slotted spoon to the broth pot and let the assembled soup gently simmer for 10 minutes.

Serve. Ladle the broth, with copious chunks of carrots, celery, and turkey, into serving bowls. Top with 3 balls per bowl, or 4 if it's for someone who picked the turkey meat without excessive complaining. Garnish with celery leaves.

Shaved Beet and Radish Salad

My friend Katie, the same genius who put the leftover turkey carcass into the stockpot on Thanksgivukkah, always brings a bevy of delicious dishes to our Thanksgiving feast. One that I always seem to ignore on the day itself is her root vegetable salad, because who has room for salad when you're angling for a double scoop of mashed potatoes?

But she always leaves leftovers, and that salad is just right on Black Friday. It's an antidote to all the rich food of the previous evening and a bright counterpoint to a steaming bowl of turkey soup.

This salad will taste good no matter what beets and radishes you use, but for the most visually dazzling presentation, avoid red beets, which stain everything they touch, and try like hell to find watermelon radishes. They add spectacular dashes of color to the dish.

Makes 8 servings

¾ cup raw walnuts

¼ cup extra-virgin olive oil

3 tablespoons apple cider vinegar

2 tablespoons light brown sugar

Kosher salt

1 pound beets (preferably Chioggia or golden), peeled and thinly sliced on a mandoline

1 pound radishes (preferably watermelon, black, French breakfast, or globe), thinly sliced on a mandoline

½ pound carrots, peeled and thinly sliced on a mandoline

¼ cup crumbled goat cheese

Roughly chopped fresh tarragon, for garnish

Toast the walnuts. Preheat the oven to 350 degrees F. Spread the walnuts in a single layer on a rimmed baking sheet, and toast until they just begin to brown, 10 to 15 minutes. Let cool, roughly chop, then set aside. ▶

Prepare the dressing. In a medium bowl, whisk together the olive oil, vinegar, and sugar. Season to taste with salt.

Assemble the salad. In a large serving bowl, toss the beets, radishes, and carrots with the walnuts and the dressing. Garnish with goat cheese and tarragon.

Substitutions and Notes: The soup will work just as well with a roasted chicken carcass as it does with turkey. Since chickens are much smaller, consider halving all the other ingredients. For the salad, the only way the beets will work raw is if they're sliced paper thin, preferably using a mandoline. If you don't have a mandoline, slice the beets as thinly as you can, then blanch them in salted water for 2 minutes.

Pairing: Soups and salads in general are not the easiest foods to pair with wine. This particular soup—with dark turkey meat and eggy schmaltzo balls—doesn't make it any easier. What you need is a versatile wine, and when I think about wine versatility, my mind goes to two categories: sparkling wines and Rosés. This month, opt for whatever bottles of Tavel Rosé didn't get chugged as Thanksgiving wore on. It has the heft to stand up to the richer elements while still retaining enough delicacy to not overwhelm the broth or the salad.

MONTLOUIS SEC

WHAT	Dry white wine made from the grape variety Chenin Blanc
WHERE	The Loire Valley of France, in an area bordered by the Loire River to the north and the Cher River to the south
WHY	This next-door neighbor to more famous Chenin Blanc appellations Vouvray and Savennières offers similar quality at more compelling prices.
PRONUNCIATION	*mon-loo-wee sek*
HOW MUCH	Decent examples cost $20 to $35.
PAIR WITH	A crab cake long on crab and short on filler

Montlouis Sec

Chenin Blanc is among the most beautiful white varieties in the world, and arguably the most versatile. It makes thrilling sparkling wines, and as still wine runs the gamut from bone dry to sticky sweet. The only other white grape that provides such quality across this much stylistic diversity is Riesling, but the flavor components are completely different. Riesling is all about summer fruits—tangerines and limes, peaches and nectarines—while Chenin is cold weather through and through, its signature fruit note one of bruised storage apples kept in a cool cellar.

For the finest Chenin Blanc in the world (with apologies to South Africa, which has adopted the grape as its flagship white variety and which is producing better and better Chenin with each passing year), we turn to the Loire Valley of France. The two best-known Loire regions for Chenin are Vouvray and Savennières, but by this point, you know I'm not going to recommend the popularity-contest winners and their corresponding price premiums. Instead, we'll look to a neighboring appellation: Montlouis.

These neighboring regions often represent some of the best values in French wines. Many of the legal boundaries were drawn up decades ago, and their relationships to actual demarcations of quality can be spotty. Take a vineyard just inside Châteauneuf-du-Pape (original boundaries established in 1923) and compare it to its neighbor across the border. Wines from the first get the CdP label and the right to price accordingly; wines from the second are labeled "Côtes du Rhône" and cost $10. In the Loire Valley, there is a river (the Loire itself) separating Vouvray (established 1936) and Montlouis (1938), but otherwise the two regions are quite similar: similar soils, identical climate, shared obsession with Chenin Blanc. The difference is that one region is well established, the other an up-and-comer. The value is always in the comers.

The soil that Vouvray and Montlouis share is called *tuffeau*, the fine-grained limestone of the Loire Valley, exceptional for vineyards. Many of the chateaus of the region (you know, the ones incessantly featured on the Viking River Cruises ads on PBS; we get it, can we please just watch

169

Downton Abbey now?!) are built out of *tuffeau*, and the excavation pits are often turned into perfect temperature-controlled wine cellars. It's a handy rock. The soils on the Montlouis side of the river are marginally sandier than those of Vouvray, and the resulting wines often display a more insistent earthy side, a minerality that is the perfect foil to Chenin's ripe apple fruit.

You can find plenty of sparkling Montlouis (amid the current bubbly craze, a full 30 percent of Montlouis fruit is now produced in sparkling form), and some off-dry or sweet versions (often labeled *"demi-sec"* or *"moelleux"*), but the most typical Montlouis is still and dry (look for *"sec"* on the label) and transfixing.

Washington State Red

December is the time of year when thoughts turn to big, rich wines: winter warmers to combat the chill of long nights, robust reds to pair with beefy holiday roasts. Our default as Americans for this type of wine is California, and that's no surprise, as it still produces the lion's share of all American wine (about 85 percent). Second on that list, at about 5 percent, is Washington State, the American wine frontier.

Because Washington doesn't have the brand cachet of California, producers have to compel with value instead. What I love about this wine-growing region is that it shares California's versatility—its mix of soils, microclimates, and varieties—but it does so at cut-rate pricing. Washington is also considerably farther north than you may realize—the entirety of the state is north of Montreal—and that means excessive differences between daytime temperatures and nighttime temperatures during the summer growing season. Those large diurnal shifts help retain beautiful natural acidity in the finished wines, adding balancing freshness to the plush texture of Washington reds.

This is still a young region by world standards (the modern era of Washington winemaking is about fifty years old) and feels very much like

WASHINGTON STATE RED

WHAT	Dry red wine made from any number of red grape varieties or blends
WHERE	Washington State in the United States
WHY	While California still produces the lion's share of American red wine, Washington is quickly establishing a reputation as a source for exceptional value.
HOW MUCH	Decent examples cost $15 to $30.
PAIR WITH	A spicy, beefy bowl of chili

the science lab of American winemaking. New vineyards are being planted all the time, and there is constant experimentation with which varieties work best in which places. Washington has a solid history of producing outstanding Cabernet Sauvignon and Bordeaux-style blends (blends of Cab, Merlot, Cabernet Franc, Malbec, and Petit Verdot). Merlot is an outrageous value, offering depth and chewy tannic structure rarely seen outside the right bank of Bordeaux. In recent decades, Rhône varieties like Syrah and Grenache (and blends of the two) have gained momentum, with Syrah often expressing wonderful savory tones—bacon fat and olive and nori—to complement a core of plush berry fruit.

Are you thinking of Nirvana-era Seattle right now and wondering how grapes grow in this rain- and coffee-soaked region? They don't. The vast majority of Washington grapes are grown not in the Seattle-centric western side of the state, but in the arid desert east of the Cascade crest. That landscape, defined by cataclysm, is fascinating ground for vineyards. As the last ice age receded 15,000 years ago, the ice dam containing massive Glacial Lake Missoula (in present-day Montana) failed, sending walls of water across Eastern Washington at eighty miles per hour. The flood flowed and crashed, eddied and whirlpooled, and all along the way dragged and deposited glacial soils in a variety of formations. Most of Washington's vineyards are planted on these glaciofluvial flood deposits, and those that aren't are generally planted above the flood line on basalt soils from ancient volcanic eruptions (even more cataclysm). Don't you love contemplating the fires and floods of geological mega-events in the safety and cozy comfort of a warm December home? Trust me: it's even better with a Washington red in hand.

As usual, because we live in America, land of the free, home of the sixteen brands of Greek yogurt, we have dozens of different options for tools to open wine bottles when one will do. Let's focus on pulling corks (because if you need advice on how to open a screw cap, you may have bigger problems than this book is equipped to address). And I mean still wines. A sparkling wine cork is its own beast, but the advice boils down to: twist the cork gently while pulling up. Whether you press the cork down while twisting and aim for a gentle "shhhhh" like a badass sommelier, or give the bottle a swift shake and shoot the cork out like you just won the World Series; that's your business.

First, some brief words on what you shouldn't be using.

Don't use a double-armed "butterfly" corkscrew. They almost universally have heavy-gauge screws that shred sensitive corks. They're also bulky and look like unattractive robots.

Don't use the T-shaped twist-and-pull corkscrew. You're going to break the cork, and you're going to overexert yourself while doing so.

Don't use the two-pronged "ah-so" cork puller, unless you have a collection composed entirely of nice bottles that are thirty or more years old with crumbling corks. In which case please invite me over.

Don't use the Rabbit-style opener or a countertop contraption. Unless you own a wine bar and need to open like forty-seven bottles each night. Otherwise you're going to look like a member of a wine enthusiast steampunk cosplay club.

Don't use electric or air pump openers. In fact, don't ever buy anything from The Sharper Image or SkyMall.

Please spend twenty bucks and buy a serviceable wine key (sometimes called a "waiter's friend"). These compact, double-hinged corkscrews (originally patented in Germany in 1882) are design marvels, packing a foil-cutting knife and a perfect twin-hinged lever into a tiny, pocket-friendly package. Buy one, learn how to use it properly (it might take three or four corks and one or two YouTube videos), and declutter your kitchen drawers of all other wine-opener esoterica.

CRÉMANT DE BOURGOGNE

WHAT	A sparkling wine made mostly from the grape varieties Chardonnay and Pinot Noir
WHERE	Burgundy, in central France
WHY	This bubbly is perfect in a pink-tinged sparkling wine cocktail for a festive year-end celebration.
PRONUNCIATION	*cray-MONT duh boor-GUHN-yuh*
HOW MUCH	Decent examples cost $15 to $30.
PAIR WITH	*Gougères* or any simple cheese puff

Crémant de Bourgogne

We've come to the end of the year, a time replete with reasons to celebrate. My favorite wine for celebrations is not a wine on its own, but instead a wine used in a cocktail—the Kir Crémant—made from one part crème de cassis (a black currant liqueur) and nine parts Crémant de Bourgogne. This is a variant on the original Kir (crème de cassis plus dry white wine, usually Aligoté from Burgundy) and the Kir Royale (cassis plus Champagne). I adore a Kir Royale, but at some point I realized the light-your-money-on-fire lunacy of mixing real Champagne (which can only come from the Champagne region in France) with anything. There is the cost involved (nice bottles often command north of $50), and then there is the delicate bready profile of Champagne, which is totally obliterated by the boldness of black currant liqueur.

From that point on, my bubble of choice for sparkling Kir cocktails has been Crémant de Bourgogne. There are a series of regional Crémants in France, sparkling wines that share Champagne's production method and many of its rigorous regulations. Crémant d'Alsace is lovely; so too Crémant de Savoie and Crémant du Jura. But Crémant de Bourgogne is the closest thing to a Champagne ringer, using, as it does, mostly Champagne varieties Chardonnay and Pinot Noir. It also feels true to the promulgator of the Kir, a Burgundian through and through.

Félix Kir enjoyed a busy ninety-two-year span on earth, from 1876 to 1968. He was ordained as a parish priest in Dijon in 1901, then successively promoted to curate, vicar, and canon. During World War II, he was an active member of the French resistance, with historical rumors suggesting that he helped derail German trains swindling red Burgundy wine out of Dijon. In 1945, following the cessation of hostilities, Kir was in quick succession elected mayor of Dijon at the age of sixty-nine, a post he would hold until his death. During his political life, he served the same drink at every official function, then called a *blanc-cassis*. It was meant as a way to promote two of Burgundy's finest products: black currant liqueur and crisp white wine. Skeptics note that it may have also been a good way to mask particularly poor white wine vintages in Burgundy, but the skeptics should stick to January and February, and allow the romantics our holiday fun.

We'll never know exactly what Félix Kir would have thought of a *crémant-cassis*; Crémant de Bourgogne was not created as an official French appellation until 1975, seven years after his death. But I can make an educated guess that he'd be delighted, and that he'd happily guzzle several alongside *gougères*, the bite-sized French cheese-and-pastry puffs Kir also championed.

If you're making your own cocktail at home, the most important mistake to avoid is adding too much crème de cassis, which makes it overly sweet and one-note. Ignore any naïf who pushes you toward a 1:4 or 1:5 ratio; that's a guarantee of a cocktail that will cloy and disappoint. Just a splash of cassis will do—about 10 percent of the overall liquid—and crème de cassis will store happily for months in the fridge, so there's no need to overdo it. (And if you've run out of cassis, a glass of Crémant is lovely on its own.)

Before you drink, consider offering three toasts: one to Félix Kir, to his bravery and his political-gustatory instincts; one to the cleansing grace of the year's end, the power of first remembering and then letting go of the year's trials and triumphs; and one more to good wine, its ability to inspire love and lust and fellow feeling, to loosen our lips and lighten our loads.

December Meal

Garlic-Studded Prime Rib with Beefy Potatoes and Celery Root Remoulade

BALANCING AGENT

My grandparents all died before I was out of middle school. Unlucky. But the universe acts like a balancing agent sometimes, and I got very lucky with my maternal grandparents-in-law, to whom I eventually became something of an adopted grandson. Eventually. My wife's grandfather was notoriously protective of his family. Family lore holds that he greeted my father-in-law at the front door on his first date with my mother-in-law, large butcher knife in one hand, sharpening steel in the other. By the time I came around, the intimidation factor was less overt but no less robust.

Hiroshi Noda led a remarkable American life. Born in Utah in 1925 to Japanese immigrant parents, he served in the US Army in World War II, and then had a series of fascinating jobs after the war, including one stint as a modern furniture design consultant and another one opening the first Japanese restaurant in Salt Lake City. When he found out that I was into wine, he regaled me with stories of driving to California and smuggling plum wine back into Utah in the trunk of his car, to serve as treats for his best customers.

My liking wine helped soften his initial reticence, which I believe boiled down to "no one should date my granddaughter." What helped even more was my obviously amorous feelings about his cooking, especially around the holidays. He had, over the years, created a series of family food rituals to mark the end of the year. He understood on some deep gut level the meaning-making superpower of gathering at the table. Every New Year's Eve, we would roll sushi for hours. We'd celebrate that night with too much sake, and then—cotton-mouthed and miserable on New Year's Day—turn up to Grandpa's house, where the sushi would be waiting, alongside Hiro himself, happily dipping shrimp and veggies into tempura batter.

But before all that, there were Christmas Days. Hiro would rise early to peel and grate potatoes, and by the time we showed up, the hash browns would be sizzling, alongside another pan bursting with caramelizing sausages and a large electric fry pan where dozens of eggs were gently poaching in whole milk. After breakfast, most of us assembled in the living room to unwrap presents, while Hiro remained in the kitchen, starting the work of dinner, which mostly involved unwrapping a dazzling prime rib, seasoning it, and studding it with garlic cloves. As the years went by and he noticed my unsubtle beef enthusiasm, he took to showing me the raw cut before beginning his work, like a manager in a high-end steak house. "Hope you're hungry," is what he always said. And I always was.

Hiro Noda died on January 30, 2016, a few months shy of his ninety-first birthday. My shock and sadness at his passing quickly gave way to a profound sense of gratitude for sharing a bit of time with him and deep appreciation for a life well lived. He turned the kitchen table into a center of gravity, and I was happy to spin around it for the years we had together. Now I try to honor him by creating my own kitchen gravity, and on Christmas, I honor him in a way I know he would love. I make prime rib.

Garlic-Studded Prime Rib
with Beefy Potatoes and Celery Root Remoulade

———————

Grandpa Noda was an instinctual cook, his instincts honed, I'm certain, by his years in a professional kitchen. His prime rib technique involved blasting the rib at high heat to create a good crust, then turning the oven off and letting the interior come up to temperature over many hours. The entire house would fill with beefy aromas, and we would nurse our hunger with glasses of wine and Mannheim Steamroller carols until Hiro finally called us to the table.

I never saw the man use a meat thermometer, and yet somehow the rib always came out beautifully, with gradations from just beyond rare to just under medium: something for everyone. I don't possess that level of confidence, especially not when working with a slab of beef that costs as much as a cross-country flight, so I most certainly use a thermometer. I also use a technique that is the inverse of Hiro's, one I first encountered via J. Kenji López-Alt's *Serious Eats*. López-Alt calls it the "reverse sear." Instead of starting at a high temp and then going low, you do the opposite: cook low and slow until the rib comes up to temperature, then blast it to form a crust at the last minute. The goal of this technique is a juicier, more evenly cooked prime rib. Which is great, but I'm really in it for the fringe benefit: the cupful of rendered beef fat, perfect for punching up the umami in roasted potatoes.

My favorite potato for roasting is the German Butterball. I love its deep-yellow flesh and perfect texture, which gets incredibly fluffy when roasted correctly. If your farmers' market has a potato vendor, seek this one out.

Makes 8 servings

1 (8-pound) prime rib
12 cloves garlic, peeled
Kosher salt

4 pounds German Butterball potatoes, left whole if smaller than a golf ball, cut into 2-inch chunks if not

8 sprigs fresh thyme
Celery Root Remoulade (recipe follows)
Prepared horseradish, for serving (optional)

▶

Slow-roast the rib. Preheat the oven to 200 degrees F. Cut a dozen shallow slits in the fat cap of the prime rib and insert one garlic clove in each slit. Season the rib generously with salt and place it, fat cap up, on a rack set in a large roasting pan. Roast until the center of the prime rib reads 130 degrees F (medium rare), 4 to 5 hours. Remove the rib (with the rack) from the pan and tent loosely with foil.

Roast the potatoes. Increase the oven temperature to 400 degrees F. Add the potatoes to the fat in the roasting pan, season generously with salt, and place in the oven. Roast for 20 minutes. Meanwhile, unearth the garlic cloves from the roast. After 20 minutes, add the garlic and thyme to the pan, and continue roasting until the potatoes are tender. I begin testing with a fork after 10 more minutes (30 minutes total); typically the overall cooking time is between 30 and 40 minutes. Transfer the potatoes to a warm serving bowl.

Sear the rib. Increase the oven temperature to 500 degrees F. Place the rib (with the rack) back in the roasting pan and into the oven, and blast it at high heat until the outside is browned and crispy. This takes anywhere from 5 to 15 minutes, and you should not walk away from the oven for even a second. Burning the rib at this stage in the game is inexcusable.

Serve. If you have room, you can carve the roast tableside. That's what Grandpa would do, and it ratcheted up the already-festive mood. If not, carve in the kitchen and make platters with slices of beef, a few potatoes, and a mound of remoulade. I like to have small dishes of kosher salt (for anyone who wants to season the interior of their rib) and horseradish on hand at the table. If you're serving my wife or father-in-law, please offer them a rib to hold and eat cavewoman/caveman-style. ▶

Celery Root Remoulade

Prime rib served alongside potatoes roasted in beef fat. That's a rich meal, and we want something sharp and vinegary to cut through it all. It's also nice to eat at least one vegetable over the course of the day, Santa and his cookies-only fad diet be damned. Celery root (sometimes called celeriac) is one of my favorite winter vegetables because it mimics the fresh green snap of celery, offering a reminder of summer during the darker days of the year.

Mustardy remoulade is a classic French bistro preparation for celery root. Grandpa never made this one (boiled green beans were the traditional Christmas veg), but I suspect he'd approve.

Makes 8 servings

1½ cups mayonnaise (preferably Hellmann's/Best Foods)

¼ cup freshly squeezed lemon juice

3 tablespoons Dijon mustard

3 pounds celery root, peeled and cut into thin matchsticks

2 tablespoons finely chopped fresh parsley

Kosher salt

Make the dressing. In a medium bowl, whisk together the mayonnaise, lemon juice, and mustard.

Assemble the salad. In a large bowl, toss the celery root with the dressing and parsley. Season to taste with salt. Allow the remoulade to sit for at least 30 minutes. This will give the celery root time to wilt slightly and absorb the flavors of the dressing.

Substitutions and Notes: If you can't source German Butterballs, more readily available Yukon Golds make a fine substitute.

Pairing: While you're cooking this festive meal, you should certainly down a Kir Crémant or deux. But once the prime rib hits the table, it's the Washington red that should accompany the roast, preferably a Cabernet Sauvignon, a Merlot, or a blend of the two.

Acknowledgments

I'd like to offer sincere thanks to the following people:

Everyone associated with Full Pull Wines—our list members, who have given me wide latitude to develop my wine writing over the years; our wonderful partner winemakers and representatives; Dan Turner, who set me on this path by approving an independent-study credit to develop Full Pull way back when; and especially our team, past and present—Matt Tessler, Dennis Felipe, RhiAnnon Kaspar, Emme Brown, Sam Barton, and Lindy Irving.

Recipe testers: Pat Malloy, Full Pull's steady presence; Dylan Joffe, fellow gourmand/writer; Nick Peyton, deeply woven into the fabric of Full Pull and my family; and Katie Briggs, who rigorously tested every single recipe in these pages and provided invaluable feedback and clarity. Thank you for that and for so many memorable meals.

Guy Harris and Bryan Maletis, my consiglieres.

Emily Resling, soul sister, for connecting me to *Seattle* magazine, among many other kindnesses over the years.

My longtime editor at *Seattle* magazine, Rachel Hart. You have been a supporter of my writing for years now and an indefatigable proponent of this project.

Jen Worick and Kerry Colburn, who taught me what a proper book proposal looks like. Also to Sara Dickerman, who was an early sounding board, and to Tegan Tigani, Edie Bishop, and Michael Davidson, who helped push this project over the finish line.

My first boss, Devereaux McClatchey, whose one-word feedback on my first piece of writing for him—"Ginsu"—forever altered the way I write about everything.

Two special English teachers at Springfield High School—Ondrea Reisinger and Braden Montgomery—whose infectious love of reading and writing planted a seed that blossomed to flower many years later.

Gary Luke at Sasquatch, for helping me finally understand what this book was really about, and for shepherding it from sample chapter to completion. Thank you for your wisdom and insight, and also for connecting me with a knockout team. Thanks to Bridget Sweet for guidance, Tony Ong for beauty, and Rachelle Longé McGhee for precision the likes of which still boggles.

My mother and father, the reader and the writer, for steadfast love and support. To Lenna and Solomon, for (mostly) napping on schedule when Dad needed to write.

And finally to Kelli, who took my hand in an Ithaca dive bar so many years ago and irrevocably changed my life for the better. Here's to many more years of research together.

Index

Note: Page numbers in *italic* refer to photographs.

Conversions

VOLUME

UNITED STATES	METRIC	IMPERIAL
¼ tsp.	1.25 ml	
½ tsp.	2.5 ml	
1 tsp.	5 ml	
½ Tbsp.	7.5 ml	
1 Tbsp.	15 ml	
⅛ c.	30 ml	1 fl. oz.
¼ c.	60 ml	2 fl. oz.
⅓ c.	80 ml	2.5 fl. oz.
½ c.	125 ml	4 fl. oz.
1 c.	250 ml	8 fl. oz.
2 c. (1 pt.)	500 ml	16 fl. oz.
1 qt.	1 l	32 fl. oz.

LENGTH

UNITED STATES	METRIC
⅛ in.	3 mm
¼ in.	6 mm
½ in.	1.25 cm
1 in.	2.5 cm
1 ft.	30 cm

WEIGHT

AVOIRDUPOIS	METRIC
¼ oz.	7 g
½ oz.	15 g
1 oz.	30 g
2 oz.	60 g
3 oz.	90 g
4 oz.	115 g
5 oz.	150 g
6 oz.	175 g
7 oz.	200 g
8 oz. (½ lb.)	225 g
9 oz.	250 g
10 oz.	300 g
11 oz.	325 g
12 oz.	350 g
13 oz.	375 g
14 oz.	400 g
15 oz.	425 g
16 oz. (1 lb.)	450 g
1½ lb.	750 g
2 lb.	900 g
2¼ lb.	1 kg
3 lb.	1.4 kg
4 lb.	1.8 kg

TEMPERATURE

OVEN MARK	FAHRENHEIT	CELSIUS	GAS
Very cool	250-275	130-140	½-1
Cool	300	150	2
Warm	325	165	3
Moderate	350	175	4
Moderately hot	375	190	5
	400	200	6
Hot	425	220	7
	450	230	8
Very Hot	475	245	9